Matching Models
in Education
THE COORDINATION OF TEACHING METHODS
WITH STUDENT CHARACTERISTICS

David E. Hunt
Department of Applied Psychology

Monograph Series No. 10

Ontario Institute for Studies in Education

THE ONTARIO INSTITUTE FOR STUDIES IN EDUCATION
has three prime functions: to conduct programs of graduate study
in education, to undertake research in education, and to assist
in the implementation of the findings of educational studies.
The Institute is a college chartered by an Act of the Ontario
Legislature in 1965. It is affiliated with the University of
Toronto for graduate studies purposes.

Contents

Preface

Chapter I An introduction to Matching Models   1

Matching Models in the Schools
  II A Conceptual Systems Model: an Early Matching Model   17
  III A Conceptual Level Matching Model: a Revision   33

Models in Teacher Training
  IV A Model for Analyzing the Training of Training Agents   51
  V Matching Models in Teacher Training   67

References

Figures 1 Development Stages in Interpersonal Orientation, 20
        2 Subjective Integration as a Function of Discovery vs.
           Lecture and Learner CL, 46
        3 Concept Learning as a Function of Rule-Example
           Order and Learner CL, 46

Tables 1 Summary of Three Matching Models, 12
       2 Expected Outcomes of Stage-Environment Combinations, 22
       3 Stage-Specific Environmental Prescriptions, 24
       4 Expected and Observed Classroom Characteristics
          and Optional Environments, 30
       5 Correlates and Characteristics of Conceptual Level, 38
       6 Model for Coordinating Learner Characteristics
          with Educational Approaches, 48
       7 Training Objectives, 53
       8 Training Intervention Based on Trainee
          Accessibility Characteristics, 75
       9 Proportion of Interdependent Teaching as a Function of
          Teacher and Student CL, 80

ACKNOWLEDGMENTS

Chapter I is a revision of a paper, "Matching models and moral training" which appeared in *Moral Education*, edited by C. Beck, B. Crittenden, and E. V. Sullivan, and was published by the University of Toronto Press in 1970.

Chapter II is based on two papers, "A conceptual systems change model and its application to education" which appeared in *Experience, Structure, and Adaptability*, edited by O. J. Harvey, and published by Springer Press in 1966, and "Homogeneous classroom grouping based on conceptual systems theory in an educational enrichment project," a paper presented as part of the symposium, Conceptual systems and educational research, at the American Educational Research Association meeting, Chicago, February 1964.

Chapter III is based on a paper, "A conceptual level matching model for co-ordinating learner characteristics with educational approaches," which appeared in *Interchange*, 1970, **1**, No. 3.

Chapter IV is a revised version of a paper which appeared in the *Merrill Palmer Quarterly*, 1966, **12**, 137-156.

Chapter V is a revision of a chapter, "Differential training in teacher education and its implication for increasing flexibility in teaching," which appeared in B. R. Joyce (ed.), *The Teacher Innovator*, Washington, D.C.: Office of Education, 1968, pp. 59-77.

The author wishes to thank Naomi Mallovy for her editorial assistance and Dhun Berhamji for typing the manuscript.

iv

Preface

The Hall-Dennis report, *Living and Learning,* stated:

"The purpose and programs of our educational system must be designed to meet the needs of each individual child. The implementation of this grand design will require the support of parents, teachers, administrators, politicians, and the general public."

It will also require an enormously intensified effort on the part of educational research workers so that there will in fact be something to implement. As the quotation suggests, there are many potential obstacles to the exhortation to "meet the needs of the child," but the most obvious obstacle is the lack of knowledge of how to co-ordinate the student with his educational environment.

This book describes models to coordinate student characteristics with educational environments, and describes how teachers can be trained to provide such environments. The relation between a student and the educational environment may be viewed in terms of how well they are matched for certain purposes. Matching is used here as an abbreviated term to capture the nature of person-environment relations. For example, a structured lecture may be well matched to students who are compulsive and authoritarian, but poorly matched for independent students. In this example, matching refers to the likelihood of a certain outcome – acquisition of information, for example – resulting from a certain person-environment combination. Well matched combinations are more likely to produce the desired results (based on either theoretical prediction or empirical evidence) than are poorly matched, or mismatched, combinations.

It is important to understand that matching is used here primarily as a description of the interactive effects of person and environment, and is a holding term to describe likely outcomes of certain interactions. It is not used in the active sense, "to match," although matching statements can be prescriptions. To make this distinction clear, if I were discussing computer matching in marital selection, I would be concerned with specifying the likelihood of compatibility, not with how to bring about the wedding. I will occasionally refer to the implementation of matching models, but this topic seems sufficiently important and complex to warrant discussion separately.

Each of the five chapters which follow has appeared in other publications, although in slightly different form. They describe matching models both in the class-room and in teacher training. My reason for bringing them together in a single volume is to make an intensive, concerted presentation of the matching view in several areas so that its full potential utility can be realized. The major aim is to convey the concept of matching as a way of thinking about the complexities of person-environment interaction in education.

Chapter I discusses general characteristics of matching models, obejctives, character-istics of the person, characteristics of the environment, and nature of the person-environment interaction, and describes three specific examples of matching models.

CHAPTER I

An Introduction to Matching Models

"The fundamental factors in the educative process are an immature, undeveloped being; and certain social aims, meanings, values incarnate in the matured experience of the adult. The educative process is the due interaction of these forces. *Such a con-ception of* each in relation to the other *as facilitates completest and freest interaction is the essence of educational theory."* (Dewey, 1902, p. 4, emphasis mine)

". . . we really know very little about . . . the 'match' between individual development and external stimulation at various stages of growth." (Deutsch, 1967, p. 10)

The major reason for the lack of cumulative knowledge during the sixty-five years separating these two statements has been the failure to take seriously the implications of an interactive model that coordinates the effects of educational environments upon particular types of students to produce specific objectives. Indi-vidual differences are given much lip service, and even more drawer space in the form of filed test results, yet educational planners and decision makers continue to work from models for the student-in-general. To ignore the importance of differ-ential student characteristics leads to questions about the general effectiveness of educational procedures, such as whether a discovery approach is more effective than a structured approach. No account is taken of the differential effectiveness of such approaches on different kinds of students.

This chapter takes as a basic assumption the necessity of a differential effective-ness model, or as Stern put it, "The characteristics of the student and of the educa-tional objectives must both be employed as guides in the design of maximally effective environments for learning" (Stern, 1961, p. 728). It is further assumed that the concept of *matching* provides a helpful conceptual device for considering the differential consequences of such interaction.

Lewin's (1935) classic formula, $B = f(P, E)$, or "Behavior is a function of the Person and the Environment," and Cronbach's (1957) recommendation to co-ordinate individual differences with environmental influences have been generally accepted, but specific models providing such interactive formulations have developed slowly. Probably the major obstacle to dealing with interactive effects has been the difficulty of conceptualizing and measuring both the person and the environment in theoretically comparable terms. A few approaches aimed at coordinating person-environment effects upon contemporaneous functioning may be noted: Stern's 1970 model for viewing the congruence and dissonance between the press of college environments and the needs of students; Schroder, Driver, and Streufert's (1967) use of an information processing model to predict the optimal combination of environmental complexity and the integrative complexity of the person; Kagan's (1967) emphasis on the match between the stimulus and the schema to predict subsequent response and feeling of pleasure; and Pervin's (1968) summary of studies on individual environment "fit" to account for performance and satisfaction.

Differential effectiveness of treatment workers upon different clients has also been viewed in matching terms. For example, Sapolsky (1965) demonstrated therapist-patient compatibility to be an important determinant of therapeutic out-come. Warren and her colleagues (1967) have developed a comprehensive system for planning differential treatment. It consists of different kinds of treatment workers as well as different forms of treatment for delinquents at different levels of inter-personal maturity.

The role of matching in stimulating development from one stage to another has been considered by Piaget (1932), Kohlberg and his colleagues (Kohlberg, 1963, 1966; Turiel, 1966, 1969), and Hunt (Chapter II) among others. Several authors have noted that Piaget has dealt with the problem only in general terms:

"A fourth principle, hinted at but not quite formulated by Piaget concerns the role of the still poorly understood factor of the match between the schemata within the organism and the circumstances of the situation in determining whether accommo-dative modification will occur in any given encounter with the environment."
(J. McV. Hunt, 1961, p. 259).

Kohlberg stated (1966) the problem as follows:

"There is also an important problem of match between the teacher's level and the child involved in effective moral communication. Conventional moral education never has had much influence on children's moral judgement because it has dis-regarded this problem of developmental match" (p. 24).

Using Kohlberg's theory of stages of moral development, Turiel stated (1969):

"It is thus necessary to consider what the child responds to in the environment as well as the nature of interaction with the environment which leads to change. The effectiveness of environmental influences largely depends on the match between the level of concepts being encountered and the developmental level of the child" (p. 99).

2

Chapter II describes a model to predict the potential match-mismatch of certain person-environment combinations. This matching model specifies the environment most likely to produce developmental progression for a person at a given stage of development.

This present chapter will describe a metatheoretical framework within which matching models can be considered, and will then apply it to a few selected models. The framework for considering matching models will be organized around four major dimensions of variation: desired change, conception of the person, conception of the environment, and conception of the interactive process. Since there are not a large number of matching models at present we will occasionally use an example from research studying general effects rather than differential, or matching, effects.

DESIRED CHANGE

Matching models are designed to produce different kinds of change. The purpose of one model may be to induce developmental growth, while another may attempt to change specific behavior. Different combinations of person and environment are required to produce such different objectives.

Specific Objectives

Among psychologists, Kohlberg has been the most articulate advocate of the developmental approach in moral education (1966). His is what might be called a *genotypic* approach, emphasizing the underlying processes and structural organization which determine moral behavior. He stated the objectives of moral education as follows:

"This alternative is to take the stimulation of the development of the individual child's moral judgment and character as a goal of moral education, rather than taking as its goal either administrative convenience or state-defined values. . . . Each of the Kohlberg stages of moral judgment represents a step toward a more genuinely or distinctly moral judgment. We do not mean by this that a more mature judgment is more moral in the sense of showing closer conformity to the conventional standards of a given community. We mean that a more mature judgment more closely corresponds to genuine moral judgments as these have been defined by philosophers" (pp. 19, 21).

Kohlberg therefore adopts moral maturity as the dimension of change to serve as the goal of moral education. A person's stage of moral development is related to his moral behavior (Kohlberg, 1965), but Kohlberg assumes that the stage of moral judgment is a more meaningful unit than a single index of moral behavior or of its conformity to certain standards.

In contrast to genotypic objectives are *phenotypic* objectives which deal with producing immediate, observable changes. Although not a matching model, Bandura and McDonald's approach (1963) specified behavioral change as an objective. Following learning theory tradition, these investigators attempted to produce change in verbal behavior, or more specifically, they determined whether a child's interpretation of an event was based on objective responsibility (amount of damage) or subjective responsibility (intention of person).

3

The genotypic-phenotypic distinction can also be seen in the area of psychotherapy, where some methods are designed to produce cognitive and affective reorganization (genotypic), while other methods are directed toward behavior modification (phenotypic). The distinction can also be observed in education in that the genotypic approach aims for structural reorganization and process learning, while the phenotypic approach aims for the acquisition of specific, correct responses.

The genotypic-phenotypic distinction has been drawn in a rather oversimplified way, for emphasis. Both approaches are necessarily concerned with behavior, but they take a different stand on the role of behavior in defining objectives. In the treatment and control of delinquent youngsters, for example, one cannot ignore the frequency of reported unlawful behavior. However, there is considerable difference of opinion as to whether one should attempt to suppress delinquent behavior directly, or to deal with factors within the individual which determine such behavior. For example, I attended a conference on models for providing differential treatment for delinquents (described in Warren, 1966). One participant suggested that the best procedure for reducing the incidence of one form of delinquency, in this case, car theft, was to institute national legislation requiring wheel locks on all automobiles. This is an extreme example of the phenotypic approach which attempts to manipulate directly the occurrence or non-occurrence of a specific behavior. On the other hand, programs such as those of Warren and her colleagues (to be described in a later section), which aim to change the orientation of the individual youth, exemplify the genotypic objective.

One needs several behavioral referents to index genotypic structure. Tomkins and Miner (1957) pointed out that behavioral referents vary considerably in their "non-diffuseness," or the degree to which they provide a direct index of an underlying characteristic. Although seemingly apparent, this point is rarely acknowledged by advocates of the phenotypic approach. In commenting on the Bandura and McDonald study, Turiel (1966) pointed out that they focused on only one behavioral index, objective – subjective responsibility, of the eleven behavioral indices suggested by Piaget for heteronomous orientations. Further, he continued:

"By studying only one dimension as manifested in children's choices between two alternatives Bandura and McDonald dealt with isolated surface responses, and not with the concept of stage or mental structure" (p. 617).

Criteria for Change

Although they should be applicable to evaluating deliberative intervention in both laboratory and everyday life situations, criteria for change are especially important for evaluating the results of laboratory simulations and analogs. Sanford (1965) decried the tendency in psychological experimentation toward increasingly trivial, meaningless investigations which are irrelevant to human problems. I would argue that a major reason for this tendency is the failure to adopt criteria for change that can be applied to the results of experiments which purport to produce change.

Reviewing studies that claim to increase the incidence of so-called "self-reinforcement" (considered an analog for the internalization of self-control), Katz (1967) pointed out:

4

"Thus two criteria for judging whether a particular type of socially learned behavior has become internalized would be (a) whether it occurs in the absence of direct or indirect surveillance, and (b) whether it occurs in the absence of any external mediation of immediate affective consequences" (pp.155-156).

He continued by noting that none of the studies up to that time which purported to increase "self-reinforcement" had met earlier criteria.

Following Piaget, Kohnstamm (1966) has summarized five criteria for evaluating a newly acquired behavior. Piaget had originally proposed that the newly acquired behavior should be "(1) lasting, (2) transferable, and (3) fundamentally different from the pre-experimental level of behavior" (p. 4). Kohnstamm added (4) difficulty of acquisition (presumably on the basis that nothing which comes easily will last), and (5) resistance to extinction.

Closely related to these criteria is the view of how change occurs. Kelman (1961) has described "Processes of opinion change," and his conception of change through compliance is similar to the process assumed to occur in the phenotypic approach:

"Compliance can be said to occur when an individual accepts influence from another person or from a group because he hopes to achieve a favorable reaction from the other. He may be interested in attaining certain specific rewards or in avoiding certain specific punishments that the influencing agent controls" (p. 62).

Kelman's description of the process of internalization is similar to the genotypic approach:

"Internalization can be said to occur when an individual accepts influence because the induced behavior is congruent with his value system. It is the content of the induced behavior that is intrinsically rewarding here. The individual adopts it because he finds it useful for the solution of a problem, or because it is congenial to his own orientation, or because it is demanded by his own values" (p. 65).

To evaluate change occurring through the process of internalization thus requires multiple change criteria. An investigator may or may not agree with the criteria suggested; nonetheless, he should explicate whatever criteria he does use, so that the relevance of his results can be appropriately evaluated.

CONCEPTION OF THE PERSON

For matching models, individual differences must be expressed in a form comparable to that of environmental differences, so that statements about the consequences of person-environment interactions can be made. Most models represent the person on one or more dimensions, which vary in their relative emphasis on structure or dynamics; such representations can then be placed in relation to corresponding environmental representations.

How Personal Variation is Represented

Stage theories view the person's position on a single dimension in relation to some value orientation which assumes higher levels to be more desirable. Primary examples are moral maturity (Kohlberg, 1963), conceptual level (Harvey, Hunt, &

Schroder, 1961, Chapter II); and interpersonal maturity level (Sullivan, Grant, & Grant, 1957; Warren, 1967). Although each of these models employs one basic dimension on which to classify individuals, each also acknowledges other more complex features of individual variation. In addition to moral maturity level, stage mixture is considered (Turiel, 1969); in addition to conceptual level, degree of openness is considered (Chapter II); and in addition to interpersonal maturity level, behavioral subtype is considered (Warren, 1967).

Another group of models is that which represents the person in multidimensional terms, usually either by way of a circumplex or a profile. For example, Stern (1970) represents the person in terms of thirty psychological needs, organized in a circumplex, Schutz (1958) represents the person in terms of three interpersonal needs (inclusion, affection, and control), which are expressed in terms of a profile. Many other systems of characterizing individuals in multidimensional terms have, of course, been proposed, but these two examples illustrate the major forms of multidimensional representation which have been used in matching models.

In addition, Pervin (1968) has proposed a system which characterizes the person in terms of the relation between his present self-rating and his ideal self. He uses the disparity between these two dimensions as the essential ingredient to formulate the "best-fit" prediction for certain environmental encounters.

Perhaps the simplest representation is a nondimensional, categorical classification into a typology, e.g. dominant or submissive. As the examples illustrate, these types are frequently end points on a dimension.

Kind of Personal Variation Considered
Although the distinction is somewhat arbitrary, most models vary in the degree to which they emphasize structural and organizational characteristics (for example, cognitive complexity, perceptual differentiation) or dynamics (for example, interpersonal attributes, needs, motives). The distinction is especially important because, if the person is represented in terms of structural organization, then the environmental representation should be expressed in similar, or at least comparable, terms. For example, Schroder, Driver, & Streufert described the person in terms of his integrative complexity, and developed a matching model by placing this measure of the structural complexity of the person in relation to environmental complexity. Conversely, a dynamically oriented system such as that of Stern (1970), which represents the person in need terms, views interplay with the environment as represented in terms of press, or potential for need gratification.

The interpersonal maturity level classification of Warren and her colleagues (1966) used indices of perceptual differentiation and indices of independence and need for peer approval as referents for classification. This attempt to take account of both structure and dynamics makes the task of environmental coordination more difficult, but it also has the advantage of viewing the person as a unified organism with both structural and motivational features.

Potential for Change
In addition to representing the person's present position on one or more dimensions, it is also important to characterize his potential for change, or malleability.

6

The belief that culturally disadvantaged adolescents are irreversibly closed to further development has been expressed by Bettelheim (1964), and challenged by Deutsch as follows:

"In other words, the older child may still be malleable, but may require a very different kind of intervention strategy in order to promote differential growth" (p. 10).

Deutsch's position emphasizes the importance of both specifying potential for malleability and indicating the specific form of environmental match required.

In the absence of measures of potential for change and evidence for their validity, the danger is that the belief in the non-malleability of an individual will become a self-fulfilling prophecy (Hunt, 1966). One promising avenue for approaching the potential for change is Turiel's (1969) use of stage mixture, or the degree of variability in stages. He implied that high stage mixture, or high variability is an index of high change potential, while low stage mixture, or consistency, indicated a low potential for change.

In conclusion, even though it appears that the dimension on which a person is represented should be the same as the dimension on which change is desired, this need not be the case. One dimension may be used to represent the person who is the object of change, though change in quite a different dimension is derived. For example, it may be that a matching model based on the interaction between needs of a person and press in the environment will produce changes in moral maturity. The point may be debatable, and is of course open to empirical investigation; however, it seems advisable at this point to maintain that there is no logical necessity for using the same dimension in representing the person as that along which change is desired.

CONCEPTION OF THE ENVIRONMENT
How Environmental Variation is Represented
Pervin (1968) put the question as follows: "Should one consider the perceived or 'actual' environment?" (p. 65). One may decide on theoretical grounds that study of the perceived environment is the more promising, but discover that it contains more methodological disadvantages than study of the absolute environment. Thus one may agree with Kagan's (1967) urging the "need for relativism" in his emphatic statement:

"Man reacts less to the objective quality of external stimuli than he does to categorizations of those stimuli" (p. 132).

Although the questions arises as to how one is to measure this categorization (or what Lewin called the "psychological life space"), methods are available for measuring the perceived environment. One example is the characterization of college environments, in which as Pervin pointed out, one may obtain a relativistic, phenomenological index, by asking students for their perceptions of their college environment. In contrast, one may also obtain an absolute, objective index by direct observation and by examination of demographic data.

Another dimension of environmental variation is the degree of responsiveness of the environment, or the extent to which the person can modify the environment. Another way of stating this variation is in terms of unilaterality-interdependence (Harvey, Hunt, & Schroder, p. 119). A unilateral environment is defined as "subject learns to look externally for criteria to fit into absolutistic schemata" (p. 119), while the definition of an interdependent environment is "subject learns to view own behavior as causal in concept formation and information appraisal."

Environmental units vary in size from those as broad as an entire culture to those as minute as a pinpoint of light. Educational environments also vary over a dimension of size, ranging through educational institution, program approach, curriculum, mode of presentation, and specific lecture statement. Similarly, environments may take account of a variety of time spans. Thus, one may analogically consider the psychological climate over a long period of time, or the psychological weather at a specific point in time.

The time unit during which the match is thought to operate is especially important because, as the interactive match produces effects, the person himself may change, and the match is therefore no longer appropriate. Therefore, the model should contain some procedure for updating the state of the person so that the environment can be progressively modulated in an appropriate fashion.

Kind of Environmental Variation Considered

Conceptions of the environment vary in their relative emphasis on the content presented or the form of presentation, a distinction which is especially important in educational intervention. Perhaps it will turn out to be the case that the "medium is the message"; but at this point there does not appear to be sufficient empirical evidence in the area of deliberative intervention to prevent investigators from taking different stances on the relative importance of content and form of presentation. Few would disagree that the ultimate optimal environments will consist of a synthesis of appropriate content material presented in the most appropriate form. However, since we are nowhere near this ultimate state, disagreement exists on how to fuse the mode of presentation with the content. Approaches like that of Turiel (1969), which aim to increase the level of moral maturity by systematically varying both the content (level of concept on the moral maturity dimension) and the mode of presentation (one-sided argument vs. two-sided argument) provide an effective strategy.

Role of the Training Agent

First, must the prescribed educational environment include a human being? Very little is known about those conditions of educational stimulation which require the presentation by a training agent in order to be effective. With the enormous upsurge of computer automated instruction, the question will shortly become critical. Omar Moore's (1966) comments on children's differential response to the "talking typewriter" when a booth assistant was present or not are relevant.

"Of the 102 children that I have studied there have been a few who, at times, have responded so much better to a particular booth assistant, or to the nonautomated equipment, or to the automated instrumentation than they did to the other conditions, that the laboratory departed from the usual procedure of random assignment until

8

these children were able to play with pleasure wherever they found themselves" (p. 176).

Second, assuming that there is a training agent, is the essential ingredient he provides his general style or the specific environment he radiates? This is a particularly crucial issue, because several matching models in the area of psychotherapy and psychological treatment take the characteristics of the treatment worker as *the* environmental unit which varies, and is therefore seen as being matched, for certain types of clients (e.g. Palmer, 1968; Sapolsky, 1965). Several investigators have similarly focused on the natural style of the teacher as the environmental unit to consider in terms of match-mismatch potential for certain kinds of learners (Washburne & Heil, 1960; Thelen, 1967). As noted in Chapter IV, much more investigation of the limits to which training agents can extend their general preferred styles to other forms of approach is necessary before an adequate answer will be obtained.

CONCEPTION OF INTERACTIVE PROCESS: WHAT CONSTITUTES A PERSON-ENVIRONMENT MATCH?

Once the person and the environment have been represented along comparable or identical dimensions, one can then specify more precisely what constitutes a match between them by considering their relationship. Probably the major difference among those matching models which are sufficiently explicit to represent both person and environment in comparable terms is the degree of disparity between person and environment thought to constitute a match for the particular objectives. Or, as Stern (1961) put the issue:

"But what is an optimal environment – one that satisfies, or one that stimulates? While it may be true that pearls come from aggravated oysters, you can only get milk from contented cows. Pearls and milk each have their uses, and people will continue to exercise their preferences for one or the other, but it would be a pointless exercise of freedom to insist on milking oysters" (p. 728).

Variation in Person-Environment Disparity

As the Stern quotation implies, matching models which aim for developmental change and growth are likely to define the match in terms of a specified degree of disparity between person and environment. Models which aim for immediate functional objectives or satisfaction are likely to define the match in terms of congruence, fit, or no disparity between person and environment. An example of the latter approach is illustrated by Pervin (1968):

"A 'match' or 'best-fit' of individual to environment is viewed as expressing itself in high performance, satisfaction, and little stress in the system whereas a 'lack of fit' is viewed as resulting in decreased performance, dissatisfaction, and stress in the system" (p. 56).

The view taken by a matching theorist on the necessity for disparity in order to produce change will obviously be related to his concept of the role of equilibrium and disequilibrium in motivation. Current motivational theory accepts the necessity for some disequilibrium or disparity, as Kagan's (1967) statement indicates:

9

"It appears that the act of matching stimulus to schema when the match is close but not yet perfect is a dynamic event. Stimuli that deviate a critical amount from the child's schema for a pattern are capable of eliciting an active process of recognition, and this process behaves as if it were a source of pleasure. Stimuli that are easily assimilable or too difficult to assimilate do not elicit these reaction" (p. 136).

Specification of the "critical amount" is therefore a problem of central importance for a matching model. Kohlberg (1966) is explicit in specifying the degree of disparity required for a match:

"In fact, the developmental level of moral educational verbalizations must be matched to the developmental level of the child if they are to have an effect. Ideally, such education should aim at communicating primarily at a level one stage above the child's own and secondly at the child's level" (p. 24).

Turiel has experimentally verified (1966) this specification (as we will describe is the next section), and he has explicated (1969) the nature of the process underlying the necessity for a mild degree of disparity:

"One way of inducing change in moral thinking through equilibration process is by presenting the child with conceptual contradictions that activate disequilibrium. These contradictions have to be perceived by the child in such a way that he is motivated to deal with the contradictory events. If concepts corresponding to the higher mode of thought are presented at the same time the child may assimilate these concepts by performing new mental operations. In summary, change occurs when perceived conceptual contradictions energize attempts to restructure by exploring the organizational properties of the higher mode of thought" (p. 127).

As suggested earlier, those models that aim for functional goals of immediate performance and satisfaction tend to prescribe little or no person-environment disparity; while those models that aim for a more long-term developmental change tend to prescribe a greater disparity. However, in the light of Kagan's comments, it may be necessary to reconsider those models with immediate functional objectives, to discover the degree of disparity necessary to accomplish their objectives. It may also be noted that the same model may be used for specifying both short-term and long-term matches. For example, in applying the Conceptual Level matching models (Chapters II and III), certain educational environments most likely to produce functional objectives will be specified (Chapter III), while a different set most likely to produce developmental growth will also be suggested (Chapter II).

A secondary issue to deal with is the expected consequence of various degrees of mismatching. For example, the model in Chapter II will specify the expected consequences not only of the optimal environment for students at specific conceptual levels, but also the expected consequences of mismatching (or what Kagan referred to as too easy or too difficult to assimilate). The consequences of mismatching may vary from a mild worsening of performance and boredom to retrogression. For obvious reasons, it is unlikely that empirical evidence will be collected on extreme cases of mismatching, but we will later consider some evidence on milder forms of mismatching.

Relation between Preferred Environment and Matched Environment

That the environment a person prefers will be identical to the matched environment is assumed generally in areas of performance (Pervin, 1968; Stern, 1961) and psychotherapy (Goldstein, Heller & Sechrest, 1966). However, this relation must be qualified according to the matching objectives. Gassner reported (1968) that patients who were matched with their therapists for high compatibility (Schutz, 1958) were more likely to perceive their therapists as more attractive than did patients who were low in compatibility with their therapists; but the matched group showed no difference in behavioral improvement when compared to the mismatched group. In effect, the preferred environment may have been matched in relation to a criterion of patient satisfaction but not necessarily of patient improvement.

Astrove (1966) reported preliminary findings which suggested that adolescents varying in conceptual level tended to prefer educational environments different from those prescribed as matched environments in the change model (Chapter II). For example, although the environment prescribed as developmentally matched for the lowest group (who are poorly socialized and easily frustrated) is that of a clearly organized, structured situation, the students themselves preferred an environment with very little organization.

Findings such as these will need to be considered in relation to the tendency to experience pleasure in mildly disparate situations, so that the complex patterns of relations between the person's preferred environment and what is prescribed as his optimally matched environment can be unravelled.

EXAMPLES OF MATCHING MODELS

We will describe three specific matching models to illustrate how the classification system is applied. In each case, we consider the model according to the various dimensions suggested, and then report the results of at least one empirical investigation derived from each model. The three models – Moral Maturity, Conceptual Level, and Community Treatment Project – are diagrammatically summarized in matching terms in Table 1.

Moral Maturity Matching Model (Kohlberg, 1963, 1966; Turiel, 1966)

Since we have used the Kohlberg model frequently to illustrate the dimensions of personal and environmental variation, its characteristics will need only brief review. The desired change is an increase in the person's stage of moral development. The person is considered along the general dimension of moral maturity segmented into six stages as follows:

STAGE	CHARACTERISTICS
"1	Punishment and obedience orientation
2	Naive instrumental hedonism
3	Good boy morality of maintaining good relations
4	Authority maintaining morality
5	Morality of contract and democratically accepted law
6	Morality of individual principles of conscience" (Kohlberg, 1964, p. 400).

11

Table 1 / Summary of Three Matching Models

Moral Maturity Matching Model[a]

Moral Maturity	Stage Level of Environmental Stimulation					
	1	2	3	4	5	6
Stage 2	0		+	0		
Stage 3		0		+	0	
Stage 4			0		+	0

Conceptual Level Matching Model[b]

CL	Program Approach Structured	Flexible
Low	+	0
High	0	+

Community Treatment Project Matching Model[c]

Maturity Level	Treatment Worker Type 1	Type 2	Type 3
Low	+	0	0
Medium	0	+	0
High	0	0	+

Note: + = Matched   0 = Mismatched
[a](from Turiel, 1966)
[b](from Hunt & Hardt, 1967b)
[c](from Grant, Warren, & Turner, 1963; Palmer, 1968)

The telegraphic quality of this summary should be noted, as Kohlberg (1966) actually defines moral stages in terms of twenty-five basic aspects (p. 7). Kohlberg conceptualizes the environment in terms of its potential for stimulating role taking at one or another of these stages. Finally, as noted earlier, he specifies the match for producing developmental progression as an environment, consisting primarily of content at the next highest stage, and secondarily at the child's present stage.

Turiel (1966) tested the validity of this matching prediction by hypothesizing that "an individual accepts concepts one stage above his own dominant position more readily than he accepts those two stages above, or one stage below" (p. 614). This prediction is diagrammatically represented at the top of Table 1. In the experiment, a group of seventh-grade boys were first classified according to their dominant moral stage; next, they were assigned to one of four treatment conditions – one below, one above, or two above their dominant stage, or to a control group. Then all (except for the control group) were exposed to role playing, and discussion centered on dilemmas at whatever level was called for by the treatment condition. Finally, after one week they were re-tested to assess their post-treatment stage of development so that the degree of change could be inferred. Results confirmed the matching hypothesis: exposure to stimulation one stage above the child's present stage produced the greatest change.

Conceptual Level Matching Model (Harvey, Hunt, & Schroder, 1961, chapters II and III).

As originally stated and applied, the objective of the conceptual systems matching model (Chapter II) was to increase the person's Conceptual Level (CL). From this viewpoint, persons are dimensionalized on CL from a very concrete to a very abstract level.

On the basis of a rationale elaborated in Chapter III, low CL students are expected to profit more from structured educational approaches while high CL students should profit from fairly unstructured, flexible approaches.

Experimental evidence for the Conceptual Level model has been derived from its use as a differential treatment model in evaluating the effectiveness of several summer Upward Bound programs (Hunt & Hardt, 1967b). Upward Bound was a pre-college enrichment program, sponsored by the U.S. Office of Economic Opportunity for culturally disadvantaged high school students, in which the students attended special programs on college campuses for six to eight weeks in the summer. We conducted the national evaluation of this program by studying a sample of twenty-one of the total 214 programs. In these target programs, measures were administered to approximately 1600 students at the beginning and end of the summer, so that change indices could be calculated. It should be noted that objectives of the Upward Bound programs themselves did not specifically include growth in CL, but rather were objectives related to the goals of the program, for example motivation for college.

The matching model was used in this evaluation project as follows: based on the rationale of the matching model in the center of Table 1, the twenty-one target programs were first classified into two groups, structured approach and flexible approach, on the basis of their position on the autonomy scale. These two groups were further classified into low and high CL on the basis of the predominant CL of the students in each program. Student's change scores were then considered in terms of the model in Table 1 by comparing the degree of change in matched programs (structured – low CL and flexible – high CL) against the change in mismatched programs (structured – high CL and flexible – low CL). For four of the seven measures (attitude to summer program, motivation for college, possibility of college graduation, and interpersonal flexibility), students in matched programs showed significantly greater change than in mismatched programs, and for two of the remaining measures (internal control and self-evaluated intelligence), there was a borderline tendency for students in matched programs to change more. Not only did these results support the matching model, but they also underlined the importance of considering differential effectiveness when evaluating program impact. In only one case was there any significant change observable when difference in program approach was considered alone. Put another way, one must consider the program in relation to the kind of student in order to understand the nature of the changes which occur.

13

Community Treatment Project Matching Model (Sullivan, Grant, & Grant, 1957; Grant, Warren & Turner, 1963; Warren and CTP staff, 1966; Warren, 1967; Palmer, 1968)

The Community Treatment Project (CTP) is a very sophisticated, theoretically derived, differential-treatment model for working with adjudicated delinquents. For present purposes, only a portion of the CTP model will be dealt with: that aspect which provides the rationale for matching treatment workers with youths at different maturity levels. Many of the objectives of the model are complex, and differ for youths at different levels of interpersonal maturity. However, CTP is also necessarily concerned with preventing the subsequent occurrence of delinquent behavior. Indeed, some of the most compelling evidence for the overall CTP model is the finding that the failure rate (which included all revocations of parole, recommitments from the courts, and unfavorable discharge) after fifteen months of community exposure was 52 percent for the control group (who had been institutionalized) and 28 percent for the group treated according to the general CTP model.

According to the formulation of Sullivan, Grant, & Grant, (1957), the CTP model views persons as varying along the dimension of interpersonal maturity which also consists of the underlying organization of perceptual differentiation. Position on the interpersonal maturity level is segmented into stages and, for the treatment of delinquents, three stages are considered: low, medium, and high. In contrast to the first two models, an important element in environmental variation in this model is that of the characteristics of the treatment worker. The matching model between the youth's maturity level and prescribed treatment worker characteristics follows:

MATURITY LEVEL	TREATMENT WORKER CHARACTERISTICS
"Low	Type 1 – Tolerant, supportive, protective
Medium	Type 2 – Firm, conwise, alert, willing to punish
High	Type 3 – Wise, understanding, warm" (Summarized from Grant, Warren, & Turner, 1963).

Palmer (1968) has stated the rationale of matching as follows:

"Stated in general terms, the principal goal of matching is the establishment and maintenance of relationships which can be of increased relevance to the long-term difficulties and capacities of given types of youths, and which – from the point of view of the youths – can also be of increased relevance to their more immediate investments, preoccupations, and preferred modes of interaction" (p. 2).

Of course, during the seven-year period CTP has been operating it has not always been possible to match the youth and treatment worker perfectly. Palmer took advantage of this circumstance, and reclassified youths in terms of whether, according to the description at the bottom of Table 1, the youth had been closely matched or **not** closely matched. The failure rate for the closely matched group was 19 percent after fifteen months as compared to the 43 percent for the group who had not been so closely matched, a highly significant difference. Therefore, the validity of the **matching model was strongly supported.

14

IMPLEMENTATION OF MATCHING MODELS

Cronbach has summarized (1967) ways by which programs of educational instruction can be adapted to individual differences. Some matching models may be helpful for logistical problems, such as homogeneous classroom grouping (Chapter II; Thelen, 1967; Torrance, 1965). However, since the particular decisions in implementation such as the numbers in a group, depend on the situation and the resources available, it seems inadvisable to consider the issues of implementation in the present framework. However, we hope that the framework will indicate the general utility of matching models for dealing with problem areas, and that it may be helpful for considering the differential utility of specific matching models.

The model described in Chapter II, as the title indicates, is an early version of a matching model, based on work during 1960–1965. It is included here to give some idea of how the revised model, described in Chapter III, was developed during the past ten years. Chapter II describes the rationale and nature of the model, with an example of its application.

CHAPTER II

A Conceptual Systems Model: An Early Matching Model

In the analysis of the educational process, one must first set the major goals, then specify the short-term goals or intermediate stages that the student must reach along the way to the major goals. These goals serve as the framework to derive those educational environments most likely to produce conditions through which a student is likely to reach them. Therefore, a theoretical model should serve as a guide in setting long-term goals, it should specify short-term goals, and suggest procedures for attempting to reach these goals. This chapter first briefly sets forth a Conceptual Systems model, next suggests its specific relevance for coordinating educational environments and students, and finally describes an exploratory study in which the model served as the basis for forming homogeneous classroom groups.

The application of a theoretical model may provide a more effective approach to certain practical problems, but it also provides information for evaluating the utility of the model. In addition, one of the ultimate criteria of a psychological theory is its potential for producing change.

Following the definition in Chapter I, the model proposed here will suggest a set of conditional statements, indicating the environmental conditions appropriate for a particular person in order to produce a desired change.

The issue is not which environment is best, but rather which environment is best for a particular person to produce a specific effect. That educational environments such as a highly organized or a completely free classroom are differentially effective with students of varying personalities, abilities or whatever, is widely recognized. In this chapter we will attempt to coordinate or match the environment and person most effectively through use of a theoretical model. Although the model is potentially

17

applicable to any area such as rehabilitation or psychotherapy in which a training agent attempts to produce a desired change, we will only be concerned here with its relevance to educational planning.

THEORETICAL MODEL

The basic unit is the conceptual system defined as "a schema that provides the basis by which the individual relates to the environmental events he experiences" (Harvey, Hunt, & Schroder, 1961, pp. 244-245). A system characterizes the organizational structure through which a person processes information or "reads" events. It is concerned with how information is processed not with the content of the information. Systems also have an important interpersonal component in that they characterize the form of self-other relatedness or interpersonal orientation: how the person conceptualizes himself, others, and the relationship between himself and others.

Systems vary, from a form in which both self and others are undifferentiated parts of the generalized standard, to a structure in which the self is part of a highly differentiated others, all of which are integrated into a whole. The dimension along which this variation occurs may be considered integrative complexity, interpersonal maturity, degree of abstractness, or conceptual level. Higher conceptual level is associated with: "lower stereotypy and greater flexibility in the face of complex and changing problem situation, toward greater creativity, exploration behavior, tolerance of stress, etc." (Harvey & Schroder, 1963, p. 134). In interpersonal terms, the higher conceptual levels are associated with greater self-understanding and empathic awareness of others.

Desired Change

The first requisite of a matching model is to establish the long-term goals characterizing the desired state. To aim for general improvement is insufficient; the model must be explicit about the assumed desired state toward which the intervention is aimed. According to Conceptual Systems theory, abstract, conceptual structure and its associated characteristics of creativity, flexibility, stress tolerance, and broad-spectrum coping power is a desirable, adaptive state. This value assertion stems from a concern with the person's capacity to adapt to a changing environment. "In stressing adaptability to change we have been less concerned with the level of performance in a relatively constant environment. . . . Conceptual evolvement is described in terms of increasing effectiveness of adaptability to change" (Harvey, Hunt, & Schroder, 1961, p. vi).

A similar valuation of the capacity to deal effectively with change is seen in the following comment by Brogan (1960) who speaks of the goals of education: "What can it do? First of all, I think in the present crisis it should not educate the pupil 'for the world he is going to live in'. We don't know what kind of world he is going to live in; all that we can be certain of is that during a normal lifetime, the world will change in ways we can't now foresee" (p. 79). Therefore, when we speak of induced change or modification, we will refer to intervention with the ultimate aim of increasing conceptual level.

Stages in Conceptual Development

Conceptual development is a continuous process which, under optimal conditions

18

evolves in a given order to the highest conceptual level. We analyze this continuous process in stages or segments, as one might represent a motion picture sequence by selecting representative still shots from the sequence. The present view is based generally on an earlier statement (Harvey, Hunt, & Schroder, 1961), but is more specific, especially in relation to the interpersonal, or self-other aspects. Accomplishing the work of the present stage, or progression to the next stage, represent the intermediate goals in the present model. We segment the developmental sequence by focusing on the conceptual work which characterizes each stage (Figure 1).

The major developmental work of Stage I is that of defining the external boundaries, and learning the generalized standards which apply to both self and others. This learning of ground rules is the basic assimilation of cultural norms and expectations. When a child is articulating Stage I, he manifests features of moral realism described by Piaget (1932), in his literal concern with rules and compliance to them. Events therefore are interpreted categorically as either "good" or "bad."

The generalized standard assimilated in Stage I serves as the anchoring basis for self-delineation, the major work of Stage II. Self-delineation occurs through a process of breaking away from the standard developed in Stage I. The learning about how one is distinctively oneself provides the basis for beginning to accept individual responsibility for outcomes. This initial expression of independence may appear in exaggerated form. Nonetheless this stage marks a person's first awareness of his own feelings as cues for differential action.

The self-understanding acquired in Stage II serves as the empathic basis for understanding the feelings and experiences of others as being similar to, or different from, one's own feelings and experiences. This "empathic matching" in Stage III serves to generate a more highly differentiated interpersonal orientation. Although the person may have discriminated between others in terms of expected roles at a more concrete stage, the first awareness of others in terms of their own personal feelings and values occurs at Stage III.

The work at Stage IV consists of the integration of standards which are applicable to both self and others, enabling the person to understand both himself and others as occupying different positions on the same, transcendant dimension rather than being simply on different standards. As indicated earlier: ". . . a person need not reach the same level of abstractness of subject object ties in all areas of development. Individuals vary considerably in terms of the generality of their stage of functioning" (Harvey, Hunt, & Schroder, 1961, p. 111). When we apply the model later we assume that we are dealing with stage functioning in specific relation to the school situation.

Conceptual systems are assumed to vary both in terms of cognitive variables or information processing (degree of differentiation, integrative complexity), and in terms of motivation variables or interpersonal orientation (independence-dependence, empathic concern). For example, persons at Stage II are not only structurally different from persons at Stage I in terms of being more highly differentiated, but they are also dynamically different in terms of their greater independence.

Using a specially designed instrument, the Interpersonal Discrimination Test, Carr (1965) investigated several specific hypotheses about the pattern of self-other

Stage	Self-Other Orientation	Stage Characteristics
Sub I		Self-centered, *unorganized* phase before incorporation of cultural standards
I	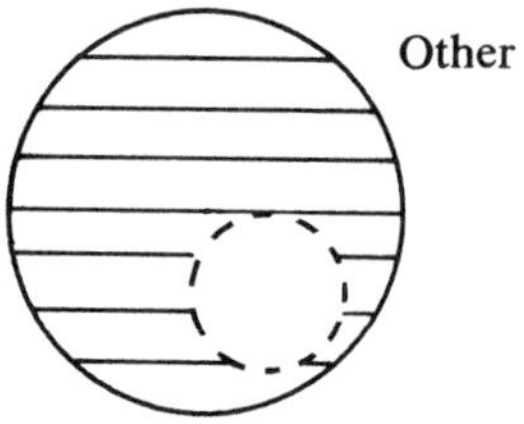 Other	Learning the ground rules or *cultural standards* which apply to everyone
II	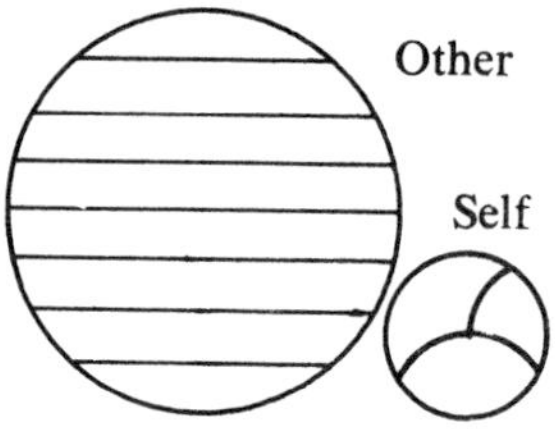 Other / Self	Learning about oneself and how one is *distinct* from these generalized standards
III	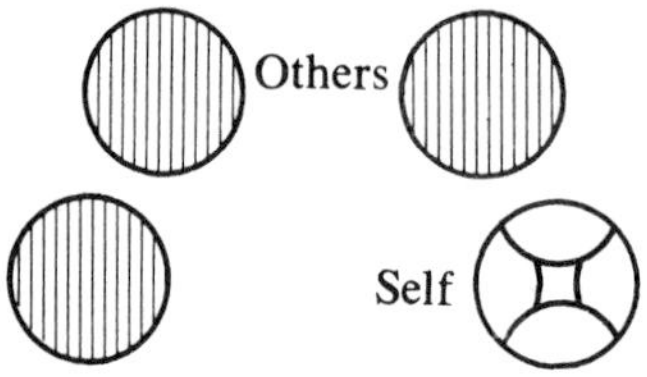 Others / Self	Applying these self-anchored dimensions to an *empathic* understanding of other persons and differences between them.
IV	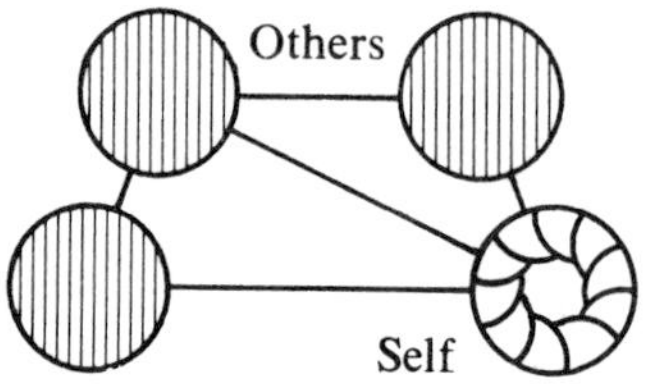 Others / Self	Placing the dimensions applicable to self and others into a meaningful, *integrated* relation.

Figure 1 / Developmental Stages in Interpersonal Orientations

relatedness at various stages. He found that self-delineation was significantly greater in persons at Stage II than for those at Stage I, while discrimination between others was significantly greater for persons at Stage III than for the lower stage groups. Thus, the pattern of self-other orientation at the three stages was exactly as theoretically predicted.

In summary, one must assimilate the norms of the generalized standard (Stage I work) before delineating oneself from it (Stage II work). Similarly, initial self-understanding (Stage II) is a prerequisite to an empathic understanding of others (Stage III). Thus, the four-stage hierarchy rests on a logically related sequence. Successful articulation of the current stage is therefore one determinant of progression; another determinant is the specific training condition. Having sketched briefly the stages in development under optimal conditions, we may now consider the specific differential effects of both optimal and non-optimal training conditions.

Person-environment Matching

The present model derives matching statements on the basis of the developmental hierarchy in Figure 1. Since the present study deals only with persons at the lower conceptual levels, we consider only environmental matching appropriate for persons through Stage II; however, the logic of environmental matching at higher conceptual levels is identical, and may be derived.

The effect of a normatively structured, clearly organized environment might encourage development at Stage I, but restrict development at Stage II. We need first, therefore, to specify the current orientation or stage of the person who is the target object of environmental intervention to determine what environments will provide a match (optimal) or mismatch (sub- or super-optimal). The match/mismatch potential of a particular environment can be viewed in relation to its effect on the conceptual work at that stage. These are summarized in Table 2. Closedness in this table refers to developmental arrestation to further progression; while openness refers to potential for progression.

To carry out first stage work successfully involves learning the ground rules of social order. Therefore the optimal environment here is a clear, consistent, well organized condition in which the cultural expectations can be assimilated. Experiencing such a matched environment leads to successful articulation of first stage structure. However, if the environment is ambiguous or inconsistent (sub-optimal) or emphasizes autonomy (super-optimal), then progressive development is restricted. Either form of mismatching produces a closed Sub I structure.

Once the Stage I work has been successfully accomplished, then the person may begin to delineate himself by distinguishing himself within the standard. The optimal environment in making the transition from first to second stage therefore is one which encourages independence within normative structure. Experiencing such a matched environment leads to successful transition to Stage II. However, if the environment is highly organized and emphasizes compliance to normative standards (sub-optimal), then a closed Stage I structure results. This specific mismatch is the frequently reported concrete functioning produced by highly controlling parents. If the environment requires too much autonomy, and removes all normative struc-

Table 2 / Expected Outcomes of Stage-Environment Combinations

Present Stage	Environment	Match/Mismatch	Expected outcome
	Clearly organized within normative structure	Optimal	Open I
Sub I	Normatively unclear or inconsistent	Sub-optimal	Closed Sub I
	Emphasis on autonomy	Super-optimal	Closed Sub I
	Emphasis on autonomy within normative structure	Optimal	Transition to II
Open I	Clearly organized within normative structure	Sub-optimal	Closed I
	Highly autonomous	Super-optimal	Transitional arrestation
	Highly autonomous with low normative pressure	Optimal	Open II
Stage II	Clearly organized within normative structure	Sub-optimal	Closed II
	Emphasis on mutuality	Super-optimal	Closed II

tures (super-optimal), then the consequences will be transitional arrestation.

Since the work of Stage II is to distinguish oneself from the normative standard, and begin to develop self-relevant dimensions, the optimal environment is one with a minimum of normative pressures and a maximum opportunity for independent self-assertion. The experience of such a matched environment leads to a successful accomplishment of Stage II work. However, if the environment is too highly structured (sub-optimal), thus interfering with the work of self-delineation, then arrestation at Stage II results. If the environment is excessively complex, in terms of the personal feelings of others (super-optimal) then arrestation will also result.

The Matching Model

This model is a differential treatment model consisting of a set of logically derived statements of the "if . . . then . . . " variety which are conditional upon the person's present conceptual level (Harvey, Hunt & Schroder, 1961). Knowledge of his level of conceptual development is essential in order to derive the specific environment most likely to produce the desired effect. Since the effect of a training condition varies so considerably in relation to the personality organization of the child, the potential effectiveness or utility of any modification procedure can be evaluated *only in relation to a child with specified conceptual structure.* The issues of which is better, foster home placement or institutionalization, permissive vs. structured education practices, disregard the structure of the child toward whom the modification effort is directed. The issue is not one of absolute superiority, but rather of the appropriateness of the modification effort for permitting maximum development of the particular child at a particular time. Although the desired state and ultimate goal is to increase conceptual level, the short-term goal varies with the child's current structure. Since progression cannot occur in a closed structure, the short-term goal of inducing openness supersedes the goal of progression. This principle is expressed as follows: If structure is closed, the initial goal is to induce openness. If structure is open, the goal is to induce progression to the next higher stage.

Although we have noted in Table 2 the determinants of arrestation or closedness, we have not yet derived procedures for inducing openness in closed systems. The major problem in accomplishing such "unfreezing" is gaining access to the person whose structure is closed. If the person is unresponsive to the environment, then environmental intervention is unlikely to produce an effect. The process of gaining accessibility is identical to that of establishing a therapeutic relationship. Therefore, the initial tactic for inducing openness is for the training agent to provide the optimal environment, with an emphasis upon his *intrinsic acceptance* of the person, a term we borrowed from Ausubel (1958) and defined as valuing the person for himself, for what he is rather than for what he can accomplish in relation to some external criterion. This acceptance of a person is always desirable, but it should be emphasized in inducing openness. Therefore, if the person is closed at Sub I, the training agent should provide a clear, consistent environment, and at the same time emphasize his intrinsic acceptance of the child. As we have noted, "the more closed the system, the more difficult the induction of structural change. The degree of extreme closedness is inversely related to prognosis" (Hunt, 1961, pp. 8-9).

Table 3 is the focal point of the present matching model. The stage-specific recipes have been transferred from Table 2, and stated in terms of prescriptions for change. Table 3 provides an indication of the environmental programming most likely to be effective for persons at various levels of conceptual orientation.

ANALYSIS OF THE EDUCATIONAL PROCESS THROUGH THE MODEL
The model just described may now be translated into educational terms by stating the goal of education, specifying intermediate stages toward this goal, and deriving educational environments most likely to help the student reach this goal.

The Goals of Education
"The goal of education in a democratic society such as ours is (or should be) to provide the conditions to produce more abstract conceptual structure . . . the role of education in our society is *not* training children to achieve higher scores on objective, machine-scored examinations. We also disagree with some prevalent views of education, especially at the college level, which emphasize placing the student in the environment that is most congruent with his existing personality structure. In our view such procedures simply promote arrestation and thereby defeat the process of growth and progression, which should be the major goal of education" (Harvey, Hunt, & Schroder, 1961, p. 340).

If a major educational goal is to encourage the development of higher conceptual level with its associated adaptive capacity and flexibility, then the present model provides a specific guide for working toward this long-term goal. The model is not, however, intended to accomplish the goal of increasing student scores on achieve-

Table 3 / Stage-Specific Environmental Prescriptions

Stage	Environment prescribed if stage open	Environment prescribed if stage closed
Sub I	Clearly organized within normative structure	Clearly organized within normative structure, with emphasis on intrinsic acceptance
Stage I	Encourage autonomy within normative structure	Encourage autonomy within normative structure, and emphasize intrinsic acceptance
Stage II	Highly autonomous with low normative pressure	Highly autonomous with low normative pressure, and emphasis on intrinsic acceptance

ment examinations as traditionally defined. A study by Claunch (1964) clearly distinguishes between these two outcomes. Comparing the performance of two groups of college students, equal in intelligence but varying in conceptual level, he found no difference between groups on traditional objective test performance. However, when performance on an essay examination which required critical thinking (and presumably therefore a more abstract orientation) was considered, the higher conceptual group performed significantly better than the lower conceptual group, as had been expected. These results underline the importance of using an outcome measure which reflects the desired objective.

Of course, the content and structure of subject matter cannot and should not be ignored; as Bruner (1960) observed, "The objective of education is not the production of self-confident fools." However, he continues: ". . . the person who thinks intuitively may often achieve current solutions, but he may also be proved wrong when he checks or when others check on him. Such thinking requires a willingness to make honest mistakes in the effort to solve problems" (p. 65). The person at a higher stage of conceptual development has more alternatives available, is better able to tolerate stress, and so is more likely to be able to cope with situations in which he makes honest mistakes.

There is some indication that the goals of education which have remained implicit for so long, will soon be brought into the open for critical examination. Educationists contradict themselves when they simultaneously give lip service to the importance of originality, flexibility, and creativity but employ procedures like teaching machines and methods of evaluation like machine scored objective tests which reward mechanistic, stereotyped responses.

As Wohlwill (1962) comments in his incisive critique of the Skinnerian application of teaching machines: ". . . in application such a prescription tends to impose, in itself, a very definite conception of the objective of the educational process, i.e. the acquisition of *particular correct responses*" (p. 143).

If, as Smedslund (1964) suggested, the outlines of the Skinner-Piaget controversy are becoming clearer, then it seems likely that such clarification will be accomplished by an explication of the opposing educational objectives, as well as of the different models of man from which they derive. In the meantime we emphasize that in order to apply the present model, increasing a student's conceptual level must be one of the major goals of education.

Student-Environment Matching

If we agree that one of the goals of education is the attempt to increase the student's conceptual level, then we may apply the present model by the following means: first classify the student according to his stage of development; then specify the optimal educational conditions for him by translating the environments in Table 3 into educational terms.

Bruner (1960) has touched on this possibility when he stated: "But the intellectual development of the child is no clockwise sequence of events; it also responds to influences from the environment, notably the school environment. Experience has shown that it is worth the effort to provide the growing child with problems that tempt him into next stages of development" (p. 39).

Assuming the conceptual orientation is known, the model may be used by referring to Table 3 for the recommended educational environment. The model can be applied to one student or to a small group within a mixed classroom. However, the most dramatic application of the model occurs when an entire classroom is homogeneous in stage of conceptual development.

The presumed advantages of homogeneous classroom grouping are well known: increased effectiveness and increased efficiency. If students are grouped according to conceptual structure, the teacher may then provide the environmental conditions most likely to produce progression for the particular group. In addition, efficiency is increased by extending the environment to the greatest number of students. The investigation of the effect of the model upon homogeneous classroom groups is an appropriate step for any approach which attempts to deal with the coordination of student and environment (e.g. Stern, 1970; Thelen, 1967; Washburne & Heil, 1960).

We turn now to consider an exploratory application of the model. Although considerable evidence is available on the contemporaneous effect of conceptual systems (Harvey, Hunt, & Schroder, 1961; Hunt, 1962; Schroder, Driver, & Streufert, 1967), there is as yet only sparse evidence directly supporting the developmental model (Hunt & Dopyera, 1963, 1964), and as far as we know, there is no empirical evidence regarding the utility of the matching model. However, one of the advantages of a logically derived model is that one may proceed more systematically through the various steps in application. Eventually, we will need to test the model by varying both stage of target object and specific educational environment to note short- and long-term outcomes. In this exploratory study we ask only simple questions regarding the potential educational relevance of grouping in terms of conceptual stage; then we will proceed to more complex questions generated by the model.

25

AN APPLICATION OF THE MODEL: CLASSROOM GROUPING BY CONCEPTUAL STAGE

The general aim of this exploratory study was to obtain some indication of the educational relevance of the model by exposing classroom groups of the same conceptual stage to the same educational environments. Students at a given stage are expected to share certain common characteristics based on conceptual level. They should respond favorably to certain forms of teaching, and unfavorably to others, even though the environments may not necessarily be optimal for progression. We expect therefore that a Stage I classroom group would differ from a Stage II group in its favorable response to a clearly structured, highly organized environment even though this condition would not promote progressive development.

In this study we ask, "Do these classroom stage groups differ from one another in expected ways?", and if so, "Do these differences make any educational sense to the teachers?" The target population was lower class students, predominantly Negro, in a junior high school in the center of a metropolitan area. This population is frequently treated as a unitary type (the culturally deprived child) rather than being considered in sub-samples differentially reactive to varying environments. Although such a population is also very refractory, the opportunity presented itself, and we felt that if a program of differential educational treatment showed favorable results for this population whose within-group variation is usually minimized, then the potential value of the model for other populations would be clearly established.

Three homogeneous classroom groups were formed: a Sub I group, a Stage I group, and a Stage II group. No explicit distinction was made between open and closed stages but probably most students of this age, in this population are relatively closed. Since the theoretical conception of these stage groups occupies such a central role in this study, we begin by summarizing the theoretically expected characteristics of each of these three stages.

Theoretically Expected Characteristics of Sub I Orientation
In the present population, the Sub I orientation is typically closed. It is characterized by a failure to incorporate the generalized standard along with an attempt to break away and define oneself. But the Stage II work of self-delineation cannot proceed without the Stage I incorporation of a standard from which to distinguish oneself. The Sub I orientation in adolescence therefore is seen as attempting to function at Stage II without having dealt successfully with Stage I. The most central feature of this unsuccessful attempt to oppose a standard which has not been articulated is *concrete negativism*. The person resists suggestion or information which he interprets as subjugation by attempting to exclude them entirely. Because he experiences inevitable failure in his efforts to be independent, he frequently manifests hostility. Because of his defective socialization, he seeks immediate gratification, and views interpersonal relations in a very egocentric, self-centered fashion.

Theoretically Expected Characteristics of Stage I Orientation
The major focus is on the generalized standard which defines right from wrong, and one's conformity to this standard. The adolescent oriented to Stage I experiences the world in categorical chunks ("good-bad"), which are based on absolute cultural

26

prescriptions. He adapts to changes in the environment only by turning to the "rule book" since for him the rules of the game *are* the game. Such inflexible concreteness, of course, precludes effective adaptation to change. Interpersonal relations occur in a network of role prescriptions, without any empathic understanding of what the other person feels or thinks. He also experiences himself primarily through a filter of role prescriptions ("What should I be doing?"), and evaluates his self-worth by his success in living up to the oughts dictated by the rules. He is highly sensitized to the status and authority of other persons, but not to their personal characteristics. Since normative standards and rules are so important, he is upset when these guide lines are unclear or when he must perform without them.

Theoretically Expected Characteristics of Stage II Orientation
The focus is on an independent break away from the standard and the development of self-anchored standards. Stage II represents "negative independence" or "freedom from" constraint, in Fromm's (1941) terms, which implies that the generalized standard has been incorporated earlier. Stage II is concerned with *self-distinctiveness,* in contrast to the concern with self-centeredness at Sub I Stage. The higher conceptual level of Stage II is evidenced by the availability of alternatives. The Stage II orientated adolescent is capable of considering self-learning as modulating otherwise negative experiences. His dislike of control is based on its interference with self-delineation; yet his more differentiated structure permits at least some tolerance of control.

Method
The sample consisted of 147 Grade 9 students. Like most samples of culturally deprived children, the mean intelligence score was lower (approximately 90) than in middle class samples. However, we are presently concerned with variations *within* this population so that the general characteristics of this target population are relevant only insofar as they qualify the generality of any results.

A battery of system-relevant measures was administered to all students in Grade 9. The battery included a theory-derived paragraph completion measure (see Chapter III) and an impression formation test (Gollin, 1958). Responses to the paragraph completion measure were scored according to degree of abstractness and negativism. For practical reasons, the Sub I group was formed from the lower half of the intelligence distribution of all Grade 9 students in this school, and the other two groups from students in the upper half of the IQ distribution. Within these IQ ranges the defining criteria for the three groups were: Sub I, low abstractness, high negativism; Stage I, moderate abstractness, low negativism; and Stage II high abstractness, moderate negativism. In addition, scores on the impression formation test which have been found construct valid (Wolfe, 1963) were used as secondary criteria. Use of these criteria led to the formation of three classroom-size groups, homogeneous in their stages of development. These groups consisted of a Sub I group of twenty students with a mean IQ of 87; a Stage I group of twenty-four students with a mean IQ of 96; and a Stage II group of twenty-three students with a mean IQ of 95.

In order to observe the different stage groups under the same conditions, each one of the groups was scheduled with the same English teacher, the same social studies teacher, and the same science teacher. Each teacher met each of the three classes daily for six weeks. During this time, eight observers recorded their impressions of the three stage groups, qualitatively and by scale ratings. After six weeks, each of the three participating teachers also rated each group, and responded to a structured interview aimed at obtaining his impressions of the groups, and how he had reacted to them with educational procedures. Neither observers nor teachers were aware of the nature of the groups during the observation period.

Observed Characteristics of Classroom Groups
The pooled observer rankings and pooled teacher rankings were in complete agreement in their ordering the three groups on the six dimensions investigated, which indicated a high degree of reliability.

Sub I group
We expected this group to be highest on noise level and interfering activities (due to short attention span), and this theoretical expectation was supported by observer and teacher ratings. Observers described this group as "noisy, poorly disciplined, generally inattentive" and "extremely resistant to teacher." Teacher comments on this group were "They get confused easily . . . they have less self control than other groups." "They really don't care what is going on . . . it's hard to keep them interested in something for any length of time beyond ten minutes" and finally, "Majority of these people are not too interested in school, period."

Stage I group
Before considering observational results, we may note that, as expected, this group obtained higher school grades relative to their intelligence than did the other two groups, even though this group was no higher than the Stage II group in intelligence. Presumably this tendency to overachieve reflects their strong concern with cultural conformity. (By the same token, if the goal of education is only the acquisition of fixed, pre-established responses, then one should aim to produce individuals with closed Stage I orientation.)

In contrast to their superior academic performance, the Stage I group was rated slightly lower than the Stage II group on academic motivation. Such an observation is not in keeping with theoretical expectation. Their first rank in competitiveness, however, accords with theoretical expectations. Observers commented on this group as follows: "The dependence on each other's approval seemed to be quite high." "Questions were asked to impress the teacher . . . group very orderly, quiet, and attentive." Teacher comments were "Anxious to make a high grade . . . never complain about the work being too heavy." "If I question them after they have made a statement a lot of them do not have faith in their convictions, and as soon as you question them they just back down."

Although the impressions given by the observers and teachers generally agree with theoretical expectations, we also observed an unanticipated interaction between two of the teachers and two of the stage groups. Teachers and observers agreed that the Stage I group functioned more effectively (higher level of motivation and spon-

28

taneity) with one teacher, while the Stage II group functioned more effectively with another teacher. We regard this interaction after the fact as possibly representing the operation of differential teaching styles which are differentially appropriate to each group (see Chapters IV and V). However, in order to investigate this interaction systematically we must measure these teaching styles objectively.

Stage II group

We expected this group to be highest of the three groups on spontaneity, and this expectation was borne out. On the other hand, they were slightly lower than Stage I on openness to information, which was not expected. However, observer comments seem to support the expected picture. Observers said: "The class interacted largely with itself, and needed the teacher only as an arbiter . . . did not seem to rely on the teacher's direction as much as the other two groups." "Interested in finding out information." "Did not ask questions to impress teacher and other students." Teacher comments follow: "They will stand up to their convictions more than (Stage I) . . . they back up their feelings . . . they will stick to what they believe" and "We had a discussion and I mentioned statistical studies done on how smoking can produce cancer, and they were not willing to believe this without checking it for themselves whereas the (Stage I) group were willing to believe it." Again, although the general impressions support expectations, there was the one specific interaction between teacher and stage group in which one of the three teachers seemed to be singularly effective with this group.

Effective Teaching Procedures for each Stage Group

In an effort to determine the potential educational relevance of the groupings, we asked the teachers "What did you find was the best way to work with this particular group?" We did not expect that the teachers would respond with the stage-specific optimal environments summarized in Table 4. We expected they would cite certain functional items as the most effective teaching procedures. As mentioned earlier, a highly structured environment may inhibit progression for persons at Closed Stage I but it may nonetheless facilitate present functioning.

The teachers described the procedures most effective with the Sub I group as follows: " . . . more visual things, demonstration, showing them the actual thing by demonstration rather than by having them show me what they know about it." "I get them busy immediately with a writing exercise . . . when it came to discussion the whole thing got out of hand, out of control" and "More rote learning, the usual slow group procedures, drilling, going over the same thing." The teacher descriptions of what worked agree with theoretical expectations. One teacher discovered that discussions did not work with this group because of their very concrete, easily distractible orientation, a comment which further corroborated our theories.

The teacher who was most effective with the Stage I group commented as follows: "This class is very competitive, so I put them in seats according to the order of scores on their tests . . . when you get a lot of competition, that's good, and they are very competitive." This teacher's emphasis on a student's position on the normative standard gives some clue about his singular effectiveness with this group. However, if progression were the goal, then the teacher should gradually introduce autonomous activities within the standard which were not so normatively evaluated.

The Stage II group should function most effectively in an environment which encourages individual activities. The teacher most effective with this group commented: "Many times I let them know how I feel about something and they'll listen to it, evaluate it, and discuss it." A summary of expected and observed classroom characteristics and expected and observed optimal environments appears in Table 4.

Table 4 / Expected and Observed Classroom Characteristics and Optimal Environments

	Sub I group	Stage I group	Stage II group
Expected characteristics of stage group	Egocentric, very negative, impulsive, low tolerance for frustration	Concerned with rules, dependent on authority, categorical thinking	Independent, inquiring, self-assertive, more alternatives available
Observed characteristics of classroom group	"Noisy, poorly disciplined, inattentive." "Easily confused, less self-control than others"	"Orderly, quiet, attentive." "Questions asked to impress teacher." "Do not have faith in their convictions"	"Did not rely on teacher's direction." "Interested in finding out information." "Stand up for their convictions"
Expected optimal environment for group	Highly structured, consistent environment providing many concrete, specific experiences	Encouraging autonomy within normative standards	Highly autonomous with opportunity for self-selected individual activities and projects
What teachers found worked best with group	"More visual things, showing the actual thing by demonstration rather than having them show me." "Drilling, exercises get them busy right away"	"Since they are so competitive I put them in seats according to order of scores on tests"	"I let them know how I feel about something and they listen, evaluate, and discuss it"

EXTENSION OF STAGE-SIMILAR CLASSROOM GROUPING

The generally favorable results of the exploratory study were encouraging not only to us, but also to the school staff with whom we were collaborating. Therefore, during the following school year, we studied the effects of homogeneous grouping in a more systematic, extensive investigation. This study differed from the exploratory study in a number of ways:

Grouping was based only on personality or conceptual stage, not in combination with IQ.

Classification into stage groups was based on two objective measures in addition to the paragraph completion measure.

Three stage groups were formed at each of the three junior high school grades so that 180 students and approximately a dozen teachers participated.

The teachers were aware of the nature of the groupings, and the matching model served as the basis for planning stage-specific lesson strategy and for weekly in-service training sessions.

Since the teachers were aware of the nature of the groups, the objectivity of their observations must be regarded with caution. However, perhaps some of the teachers' comments made in the weekly meetings will give some flavor of the relevance of the grouping procedure. "The classic example is how these groups react to our using newspapers in current events. The Stage I kids come in and they sit and wait . . . I say 'let's turn to the first page' and everybody turns to the first page. . . . The Sub I group comes in and I pass out papers and the kids look at different things, some turn to funnies, some turn to car ads, but as soon as I say 'OK, now let's look at page 1' they turn back to page 1 . . . with the Stage II group you pass out papers and you're lost, because if one kid turns to the sport page and you're working on page 1, he wants to stay on the sport page. . . . Some of the kids (Stage II), when I say turn to page 1, turn away from page 1."

Another teacher commented on the differential effectiveness of the use of a debate technique with Stage I and Stage II groups: "Today with my Stage I group I set up a debate; immediately I had three kids pro and three con, no trouble . . . but with Stage II they don't want a debate . . . you don't want to structure that or else you lose the whole thing, because everybody wants their say. . . . In Stage I you keep your discussion with a debate, in fact, it's better . . . but with Stage II you lose it because they think you're stifling them, you're directing them and this is what they don't like." We discussed with the teachers the potential value of using a debate for different groups, and how it might be adapted to meet either functional or developmental goals. Repeated use of debates, though functionally sound for Stage I, may ultimately inhibit progressive development. To encourage progression with a Stage I group, the teacher might distinguish within the options held by those who were for the issue and also within those who were against. The aim would be to teach the students to identify their own distinct opinions, that is, to encourage autonomy within normative standards.

Here are some of the comments made by the teachers about what worked best with Sub I groups: "If somebody in a Sub I group asks a question, then maybe that person will pay attention; but you lose all the others. . . . If you have them sit down with something in front of them, and you go around and talk to them individually, this seems to work best." "Everything has to be structured for them. If you put something on the board and tell them to get out their notebooks, then they will say, 'Do you want us to put it in our notebooks?' " One teacher described a procedure he hit on which we would regard as optimal for progression for students in the Sub I group: "You can bring in self-control for them even though they lack it on their own. . . . If everyone is supposed to do a lesson, some do it more quickly, and so you say, 'when you're finished, you can select either a short story or play to read'. . . . After you've given them this structure, then they can begin to make this simple decision on their own."

The teachers' impressions of the Stage I groups were consistent, and similar to those in the earlier study. Teachers working with Stage I students encountered difficulty in encouraging their independence rather than reinforcing their compliance.

31

Teachers found the Stage II group either very difficult or very challenging, depending on their own orientation. "In this stage of wanting to create, and try their own way, it's tough to get them together at the beginning of the period, to even tell them that they're going to be on their own." "Although there is a need to contain them, I would rather have a group jumping out of their seats because they are showing some motivation . . . I think it's a pleasant experience." "I find even though they give me a rough time, it's bordering on a delightful experience because they've really got you going, they've got you hopping all the time." Teachers and observers reported that students in Stage II groups frequently ask "why," and do not take teachers statements at face value. This high incidence of inquiry suggests that the discovery method, or inquiry training (Suchman, 1961) might be especially effective for them (see Chapter III).

There was one unanticipated bonus. Since only half of the 360 students were in stage-similar groups, those teachers who also taught unclassified classroom groups began to ask what the unclassified students were like and what procedures were most likely to be effective for them. Grouping students according to stages seemed to make teachers more sensitive to variations in students whether they are grouped or not.

The teacher comments are reported to indicate that the present model for analyzing the educational process is at least moderately relevant to the problems teachers encounter in the classroom; the comments are clearly not sufficient to provide the basis for objective evaluation. The difficulty of using the teachers to evaluate the effects of the program once they have become aware of its nature is a problem familiar to anyone conducting a program of controlled intervention.

The differential reactions of these students, almost all of whom would be considered culturally deprived, deserves mention. Most authors, such as Riessman (1962), speak of the culturally deprived child as a monolithic entity. In contrast, these results emphasize the importance of considering variations within the group. The study of personality variations within lower-class children not only has the advantage of understanding these children better, but also provides the opportunity to observe similarities as well as differences between them and middle-class children. Stage classification is applicable to persons of all social classes.

These studies illustrate the application of the model and suggest some results. That teachers found grouping by stage useful in increasing their teaching effectiveness may be the most meaningful index of its value at this point.

We are just beginning to evaluate the utility of the model. We will need a program of controlled investigations: to study more objectively the reaction of different stage groups to the same controlled environment; to study reactions of stage groups to educational environments varying in expected match/mismatch potential (Table 2); and to study the long-term effects of educational environments coordinated with stage groups, according to the optimal match (Table 3).

The most urgent immediate need, however, is for a method to describe educational environments in terms which are theoretically relevant, objective, and meaningful to teachers, a task which has begun (Joyce, 1964). An objective means for coding educational environments will not only permit more careful investigation of the effects of differential educational treatments, but will also open many other areas for investigation.

32

Chapter III describes the most recent version, a Conceptual Level matching model for coordinating student characteristics and educational approaches. This chapter summarizes evidence supporting Conceptual Level gathered since 1965, and describes several matching studies conducted in schools.

CHAPTER III

A Conceptual Level Matching Model: A Revision

"I suppose alert teachers have always been intuitively aware of the fact that when they change their method of teaching that certain children who had appeared to be slow learners or even non-learners became outstanding achievers and some of their former star learners became slow learners. They have also learned that when they change the nature of the test used for assessing achievement, such as from a multiple-choice test to one requiring creative applications of knowledge and decision making, the star learners may change position in class ranking markedly" (Torrance, 1965, p. 253).

Without worrying for the moment about how many teachers are in fact aware of the differential effects of various educational approaches or the differential consequences of measuring educational achievement, let us consider the implications of this statement in terms of our major assumption. If a psychological principle is to be useful for education, it should take into account both the effectiveness of different approaches upon different types of students, and the differential results from using various measures of indexing accomplishment.

To consider the differential effectiveness of an educational approach (or any other form of environmental influence), one does not simply point out a few persons to whom the principle does not apply. Nor does one consider individual differences as unwanted error variance. To take the differential approach seriously means to ask different questions and generate principles in a different form. Rather than ask whether one educational approach is generally better than another, one must ask

"Given this kind of person, which of these approaches is more effective for a given objective?".

The classic statement of the differential, or interactive approach was made by Kurt Lewin (1935) in the formula, $B = f(P,E)$, or Behavior is a combined function of the Person and the Environment. At first glance, this formulation may seem a pedantic restatement of the obvious. However, when translated into educational terms – i.e. the accomplishment of an educational objective depends upon the effect of the educational approach on the individual learner – one realizes that educational problems are rarely viewed in differential terms.

In his 1957 presidential address to the American Psychological Association, Cronbach concluded with the following recommendation:

"It is not enough for each discipline to borrow from the other. Correlational psychology studies only variance among organisms; experimental psychology studies only variance among treatments. A united discipline will study both of these, but it will also be concerned with the otherwise neglected interactions between organismic and treatment variables. Our job is to invent constructs and to form a network of laws which permits prediction. *From observations, we must infer a psychological description of the situation, and of the present state of the organism. Our laws should permit us to predict, from this description, the behavior of organism-in-situation"* (Cronbach, 1957, pp. 681-682, emphasis mine).

Despite the logical appeal of Cronbach's suggestion for an interactive approach, the development of constructs that coordinate person-environment effects has proceeded slowly. Perhaps one reason is, although the general nature of such a co-ordinated approach is quite straightforward, that the specific research strategies for developing such principles are much less clear. Cronbach has more recently (1967) stated the interactive formulation specifically for education by suggesting an "Aptitude-Treatment-Interaction" (ATI) model. In ATI one searches for combinations of learner aptitude and educational treatment that will produce differential effects. Cronbach and Snow (1968) have suggested three sources of hypotheses in the ATI approach:

"(1) derived from review of literature, (2) derived from aptitude variables of particular importance for theories of cognitive and personality development, and (3) comparisons of controversial instructional methods" (p. 9).

The Conceptual Level (CL) matching model to be described here is a revision of the Conceptual Systems model described in Chapter II. Similar in rationale to the ATI approach, the matching model aims to set forth principles that specify those approaches most likely to facilitate achieving certain objectives for different kinds of persons. In educational terms, the ultimate form of a matching model is a set of "if . . . then . . ." conditional statements specifying that educational approach most likely to accomplish a particular objective for an individual learner.

Before the matching model and empirical evidence derived from it are described, the personality dimension on which it is based – Conceptual Level – is described, and its construct validity and characteristics summarized.

CONCEPTUAL LEVEL

Theoretical Background

As described in Chapter II, the Conceptual Systems approach (Harvey, Hunt, & Schroder, 1961) viewed personality development as an interactive function of the person's level of personality development (or stage), and the environmental conditions he encountered. Optimal development was assumed to occur when the environmental conditions facilitated the conceptual work necessary for the person's conceptual growth, as described in Table 2.

It is important to note that the 1961 position was intended as a provisional statement to generate empirical investigations that would either support, or lead to revisions of, this initial position. Not surprisingly, therefore, the initial position has undergone considerable revision as each of the original three authors has worked in various domains, and made conceptual and methodological revisions that have led to derivative theories (Chapter II; Harvey, 1967; Schroder, Driver & Streufert, 1967). The present derivative, the Conceptual Level matching model, can be better understood if seen in a perspective of the original Conceptual Systems viewpoint, and its derivatives.

In the earlier model summarized in Chapter II, Conceptual Systems (or stages) were defined partly in terms of motivational orientations: Stage I – unilateral dependence, Stage II – negative independence, Stage III – conditional dependence and empathy, and Stage IV – interdependence. These hypothesized stage-specific characteristics led to the assumption that a person could be classified into one of the four stages or systems on the basis of his primary motivational concern. When a motivation-based definition is used, measurement is likely to be based on the system-specific content of a person's response, with each person being classified into one of the four relatively discontinuous system categories. Since Conceptual Systems were also defined partly in terms of structure, they were designed to coordinate the otherwise discrete features of motivation and structure. When a structurally-based definition is used, measurement is likely to be based on structural referents such as differentiation, discrimination, and integration, and the person classified on a dimension of conceptual complexity. Although systems were assumed to vary in both motivation and structure, there was no supporting evidence for this assumption.

A major difference among the Conceptual System derivatives, therefore, is their relative emphasis on motivation (or content) as opposed to conceptual complexity (or structure). During the past decade, for example, Harvey (1967) and his colleagues have emphasized the motivation or system-specific content characteristics; have used content-oriented measures (both objective and free response) for classifying persons into one of the four system categories; and have investigated system-specific hypotheses (not always hierarchically ordered) in several areas, including attitude change.

In contrast, Schroder and his colleagues (1967) have viewed personality organization as varying on a continuous dimension of integrative complexity (defined in terms of differentiation, discrimination, and integration); have measured integrative complexity by coding free responses, and assigned scores accordingly; and

35

have compared the responses of persons varying in complexity to situations varying in complexity.

It should be noted that the present distinction among the three authors is not intended to place more value on one derivative or another, but rather to set them each in clear perspective. Unless distinctions between them are made clear, and the derivative theories updated, other investigators may assume that the earlier provisional statement is still accepted and may design investigations that use the measures from one derivative to test hypotheses in another. For example, they might use one of Harvey's content-based measures to test a hypothesis in information processing according to some of Schroder's structural notions.

The third derivative position that uses Conceptual Level as the basic personality dimension is one that I have been developing, and is summarized in the remainder of this section. As indicated in Chapter II, one addition to the 1961 version was the inclusion of a very low stage, referred to as Sub I. Furthermore, on the basis of cross-sectional investigations in the twelve- to eighteen-years age range, the motivational orientation thought to characterize the hypothetically superior Stage III persons (mutuality and affiliation), did not occur more frequently in older than younger children as might have been expected. In addition, there were no persons with Stage IV characteristics. Accordingly, the usefulness of the motivationally based system-specific characteristics of Stage III and Stage IV was seriously questioned by this CL derivative. In summary, this CL derivative views personality organization on a continuous dimension, with very general anchor points at what we have referred to earlier as Sub I Stage, Stage I, and Stage II. Most of the work described here is with persons in the twelve- to eighteen-years age range. Therefore, the reservations expressed about the usefulness or occurrence of patterns above Stage II should be considered in terms of the samples studied and methods used. It is, of course, possible that higher stage levels may occur in samples of older groups.

Though the principles of construct validity clearly emphasize that such procedures involve validating both the method of indexing the construct and the construct itself, this unavoidable fusion of method and construct has frequently been overlooked. In the present work, all results related to the CL construct were based on the Paragraph Completion Method, unless noted otherwise.

Measurement of CL: Paragraph Completion Method

The various levels of conceptual development are conceived in a succession of hierarchically ordered stages outlined in Chapter II. A developmental theory, however, requires longitudinal evidence to support it. In this case, the evidence must demonstrate, not only that each stage follows the prescribed sequence, but that every person passes through each stage. The developmental rationale in the CL model is only an assumption, with virtually no longitudinal support; therefore, it should be regarded as a helpful metaphor that may or may not be valid. One can arrive at a similar set of hierarchically arranged referents based entirely on conceptual complexity, i.e. greater differentiation, discrimination, and integration. In this sense the CL dimension (and its method of measurement), are very similar to the integrative complexity derivative used by Schroder et al. (1967).

The method of measuring CL was developed to index a person's position on the continuous CL dimension, rather than to follow the developmental stage notion exclusively. The classification of persons according to their Conceptual Level may be useful for research or decision making, but it is important to emphasize that such classification is based on similarity in conceptual orientation, and does not imply that these persons are all at the same stage of development.

To index CL, we have used a method that requires the person to do some conceptual work. He must react to a stimulus likely to require some "cognitive work" in his response. Specifically, the paragraph completion method consists of six topics: "What I think about rules . . . ," "What I am criticized . . . ," "What I think about parents . . . , " "When someone disagrees with me . . . , " "When I am not sure . . . , " and "When I am told what to do. . . ." To each of these he responds with three or four sentences, indicating his own personal reactions to it.

Each of the responses is coded according to the scoring manual (Hunt, Lapin, Liberman, McManus, Post, Sabalis, Sweet & Victor, 1968). Scores from 0 to 3 indicate generic referents (see below). Specific examples are given for scores on each topic. The metric scoring is similar to the earlier stage metaphor: a score of 0 is similar to the Sub I characteristics; a score of 1 corresponds to Stage I; 2 to a transitional stage; and 3 to Stage II. The scores are also similar to those used for indexing integrative complexity (Schroder et al., 1967, Appendix 2).

Generic referents are as follows:

For a score of 0: very undifferentiated response, overgeneralized exclusion of any negative input, lack of affective control.

For a score of 1: categorical judgments, overgeneralized and unqualified acceptance of single rule, recourse to external standards.

For a score of 2: some form of conditional evaluation, beginning self-delineation, expression of alternatives.

For a score of 3: taking two viewpoints into account simultaneously, co-ordination of evaluation of situation with differential response, and clear indications of self-delineation and internal standards.

Users of the manual are encouraged to judge the underlying conceptual structure which generates the response rather than their actual content. In come cases, where the response is insufficient, the unscorable category is used.

A person's CL index is calculated as a composite of his six scores. Two procedures for aggregating scores are used: the first is a simple average of all scorable responses, and the second is the average of the highest three scores. Schroder et al. (1967) originally proposed this latter procedure which we have used in the next section. It is based on a rationale similar to the "ceiling" on the Binet test (that is, if a person scores on one or two occasions at a higher level, then this score must be an accurate referent of his underlying structure). Furthermore it must be remembered that one often gives lower level responses if one becomes bored with the task.

With trained raters, the inter-rater reliability is .80 to .85. In many of the studies reported, two judges have scored all protocols in order to sharpen precision, but it is hoped that as the manual is improved, two will not be necessary.

Correlates, Characteristics and Construct Validity of CL

The following summary is based on CL as indexed by the Paragraph Completion Method and, with only an occasional exception, using the manual of Hunt, et al. (1968). Most of the findings discussed are summarized in Table 5. Others not in Table 5 are referred under the appropriate topic.

Table 5 / Correlates and Characteristics of Conceptual Level

Related variable	N	School Grade	Results	Source
Intelligence				
California Test of Mental Maturity	206	7-9	r = .09	Hunt, 1965
Lorge-Thorndike	175	8-12†	r = .24**	Cross, 1966
Canadian Academic Aptitude Test	175	11	r = .15*	McLachlan, 1969
Scholastic Aptitude Test (Verbal)	160	College	r = .10	Pohl & Pervin, 1968
Vocabulary	1550	9-12	r = .29**	Hunt & Hardt, 1967a
Vocabulary	830	9-12	r = .27**	Hunt, Hardt & Victor, 1968
Age or School Grade				
Age	207	7-9	r = .08	Hunt, 1965
Age	175	8-12†	r = .07	Cross, 1966
School grade	830	9-12	r = .17**	Hunt, Hardt & Victor, 1968
Social Class				
Lower	277	7-9	Middle higher	Hunt & Dopyera, 1966
Middle	692	7-9	than lower	
Sex				
Girls	481	7-9	Girls higher	Hunt & Dopyera, 1966
Boys	488	7-9	than boys	
Academic Achievement				
GPA	830	9-12	r = .17**	Hunt, Hardt & Victor, 1968
GPA (with SAT partialled out)	150	College	r = .16*	Pohl & Pervin, 1968
Personality Measures				
Kohlberg Moral Maturity Scale	120	9-13	r = .34**	Sullivan, McCullough & Stager, 1970
Loevinger Scale of Ego Development	120		r = .23**	Sullivan, McCullough & Stager, 1970
Future orientation	1550	9-12	r = .26**	Hunt & Hardt, 1967a
Non-alienation	1550	9-12	r = .21**	Hunt & Hardt, 1967a
Internal control	1550	9-12	r = .12**	Hunt & Hardt, 1967a

†Boys only   * p < .05   ** p < .01

Relation to intelligence
As Table 5 indicates, there is a relation between CL and intelligence. This relation, though significant with the fairly large samples, is of a relatively low order. Table 5 gives only a sample, but it represents the usual finding; namely that in groups of fairly heterogeneous intelligence, the relation is usually in the .20's; while for more intellectually homogeneous groups, such as college students, the relation is typically positive but not significant. Obviously, in the investigation of CL effects, intelligence effects must be controlled.

Relation to age or school grade level
Since CL is presumably related to development, the low correlations to chronological age (CA) are initially surprising. When the relation of CL to age is investigated by cross-sectional analysis, the mean scores show a fairly orderly, though slight, pattern of increase from age twelve to sixteen: 1.28, 1.36, 1.44, 1.51, and 1.47, respectively (Hunt, 1964). Of more significance are the only available longitudinal results on CL (Hunt, 1968), which reported scores for a group of seventy-two boys over a four year period. At initial testing, the boys were in Grades 6-8, their mean CL score was 1.36; four years later, when they were in Grades 10-12, the mean score for the total group showed a significant increase (p <.01) to 1.54.

The most likely reason for the fairly low relation to CA in these three sets of results (correlational, cross-sectional, and longitudinal), is probably that none of these studies included measures of environmental effects. It would be necessary to conduct a longitudinal investigation that included measures of the environment experienced, to verify developmental hypotheses of an interactive nature. On the basis of these results only, it appears that during the twelve to sixteen years age range there are relatively orderly, though not very large, increments in conceptual development.

Relation to social class
The middle class superiority in CL indicated in Table 5 was not surprising. (It should be noted that the lower class sample was about 90 percent Negro.) More important was the additional finding that the lower class sample showed greater variability in CL than did the middle class sample. Proportionately more middle class students are at the low (CL = 1) level, while proportionately more lower class students are at the very low level. Surprisingly, the lower class sample contained a slightly greater proportion (almost all female) at high CL. As we noted in Chapter II, judging by these results, the lower class students should not be treated as a monolithic entity.

Sex differences
The female superiority was noted for both the middle and lower class samples, but was much more striking for the lower class sample (Hunt & Dopyera, 1966). Although results are likely to vary slightly from one sample to another, the results of most of our investigations suggest that at the high school level, the sex difference in CL is likely to have disappeared. However, as with intelligence, we have regarded

it important, wherever possible, to investigate whether the same pattern of CL effects holds for both sexes.

Relation to academic achievement

As Table 5 indicates, CL is generally, though not strongly, related to academic achievement. The more interesting results appear when one considers the content and the method for indexing achievement. The correlation between CL and Grade Point Average (GPA) with the effect of intelligence (SAT) partialled out, for twenty-eight engineering students was $-.56$ ($p<.01$), while the CL-GPA correlation for twenty-two social science students was .44 ($p<.05$), and for sixty humanities students, $r = .38$ ($p<.05$) (Pohl & Pervin, 1968). These differential results indicate that the overall correlation of .16 in Table 5 showed quite different patterns depending upon the nature of the subject matter. In the case of engineering, which presumably requires a more conventional orientation of memorization, CL is inversely related to achievement; while in social science and humanities, which presumably require more critical thinking, analysis, and generation of alternatives, the correlation is positive.

The finding by Claunch (1964), described in the last chapter, that CL groups differed only when the criterion was complex, is another reminder of the importance of considering the level required in the criterion task. The implication of these results for designing investigations of CL effects is to underline the importance of indexing achievement at different levels on the taxonomy.

Relation to social desirability

Campbell (1960) has suggested that information on the susceptibility of the measure to social desirability instructions be given. When the Paragraph Completion Method was administered under "fake good" instructions, the mean CL scores decreased significantly ($p <.05$), as compared with the same group's performance under standard instructions (Hunt, 1962). These results were interpreted to mean that the fake good instructions induce persons to respond with many responses scored 1, for example, reliance on authority, categorical judgements. This interpretation is supported by results of another investigation in which the scores on the Children's Social Desirability (CSD) Scale (Crandall, Crandall, & Katkovsky, 1965) of three groups of students varying in CL were compared. Mean CSD score for the very low group was 17.35, for the low (CL $= 1$) group, 23.80, and for the high group, 16.53 (Hunt, 1965). This curvilinear pattern suggests that what is referred to as a social desirability tendency, whether induced or dispositionally present, is very similar to a CL score of 1. It is interesting to recall the strong tendency of the students in a middle class junior high school sample to score 1 when compared to the lower class sample.

Relation to parental training conditions

Cross (1966) has studied the parental training conditions of boys varying in CL. The major portion of the investigation consisted of defining two groups of twenty-seven boys, individually matched for IQ and CA, but varying in CL. The mean of the high CL group was 2.0, while the mean of the low CL group was 1.1.

40

Both parents of all fifty-four boys were individually interviewed with a specially designed schedule, and their responses coded for degree of interdependence. The scale ranged from very interdependent and reflective to very unilateral and autocratic. When the scores of the mothers, fathers, and combined parents of the two CL groups were compared, the parents of the high CL group were significantly higher in interdependence in all three comparisons. In a correlation analysis with a larger sample (N = 175), Cross found that a boy's CL was significantly correlated (r = .23, p<.01) with parental non-authoritarianism as indexed by the Parental Attitude Research Instrument.

Cross has also recently (1970) studied the relation of parental training conditions to CL in a younger (sixth grade) sample of boys and girls. Parental interdependence, again indexed by an interview, was higher for parents of high CL children than for parents of low CL children, but the superiority did not reach statistical significance (t = 1.69, p <.10). When scores were analyzed separately by sex of parent and sex of child, the predicted relation was statistically significant only for mothers of high CL girls who were more interdependent (p<.005) than mothers of low CL girls. Although the results of this replication attempt to qualitfy the original findings somewhat, and results of these two studies cannot be interpreted to represent longitudinal causal influence, they are generally in keeping with the hypothesized type of parental background experienced by children varying in CL.

Relation to delinquency
The incidence of both observed and reported delinquency was found to be higher for boys in the very low CL group than in the group with higher CL scores (Hunt & Hardt, 1965). These findings agree with the assumed lack of organization and lack of assimilation of norms typical of the very low CL group.

Relation to other measures of developmental maturity
Sullivan, McCullough & Stager (1970) investigated the relation between CL, Kohlberg's Moral Maturity Scale (1964), and Loevinger's Ego Development Scale (1966), in three different age groups: twelve, fourteen, and seventeen. The correlations in Table 5 have partialled out the effect of age, and indicate a substantial relation between CL and level of moral and ego development.

Two investigations (France, 1968; Hunt & McManus, 1968) have studied the relation between CL and the interpersonal Maturity Level described in Chapter I, and originally by Sullivan, Grant, and Grant (1957). Although there were very general relations, the degree of correspondence was not high.

Relation to other personality measures
As Table 5 indicates, Hunt & Hardt found (1967b) CL to be significantly related to future orientation (Strodtbeck, 1958), non-alienation (Srole, 1956), and to internal control (Rotter, 1966), though this latter relation is not as high as one might expect from the hypothetical descriptions of CL and internal control. These relations were replicated in another sample of 830 students by correlations of .12, .17, and .13, respectively (Hunt, Hardt & Victor, 1968). For persons at the college

level, CL has been found to be inversely related to dogmatism and authoritarianism (Schroder et al., 1967).

CONCEPTUAL LEVEL MATCHING MODEL

The CL model will be considered according to the metatheoretical framework suggested in Chapter I for considering matching models. It consists of: desired change, conception of the person, conception of the environment, and conception of the interactive process between person and environment. In Lewinian terms, the four aspects are B,P,E and P-E interaction, respectively. In educational terms, these four aspects are educational objectives, learner characteristics, educational approaches, and theory of instruction, respectively.

Desired Change (Educational Objectives)

When the CL matching model is applied to education, the objectives can be conceived in terms of two widely used taxonomies, cognitive (Bloom, 1956) and affective (Krathwohl, Bloom & Masia, 1964). Matching predictions will vary according to the particular objective. For example, it seems likely that for such objectives as recall and memorization, CL-treatment interactions are unlikely; while for more complex objectives, interactions may be expected. Although very little is known about the relation between cognitive and affective outcomes, it seems important to include both wherever possible, in order to learn more about their interrelation and their differential susceptibility to matching.

A major dimension of variation in objectives described in Chapter I is that of phenotypic vs. genotypic. Phenotypic objectives are defined as short-term changes in behavior that are unlikely to generalize either over space (to other content areas) or time (resist extinction). Genotypic goals, on the other hand, or what Schroder (1970) has called "process" goals, involve more enduring structural reorganization. Genotypic objectives are exemplified by problem-solving strategies and learning sets. A major reason why genotypic objectives have not been more widely adopted is that they are much more difficult to measure. It may also be, as some have recently suggested, that they are difficult, if not impossible, to attain. It seems clear that we cannot approach the question until adequate indices of genotypic educational objectives are available.

Conception of the Person (Learner Characteristics)

Personal variation is considered on the CL dimension, which is thought to represent conceptual complexity and related characteristics previously summarized. Specific person-environment hypotheses will be developed based on the person's position on the CL dimension; that is, given a person with a specified level of information processing capacity, what educational approach is likely to be most effective?

A person's CL may be considered as either cause or effect. In this revised matching model and the work derived from it, we have considered learner CL as the cause, or what we describe later as an *accessibility channel*. CL in this sense is thought of as a fairly stable characteristic. However, this view should not indicate that it is no longer valuable to attempt to increase learner CL through deliberative

42

educational intervention as proposed in Chapter II. Cronbach & Snow (1969) have referred to this paradox in relation to aptitude as follows:

"Work on personality will have continually to contend with the technical and philosophical problems that arise from the fact that 'aptitude' may be a predictor, an intervening variable arising from the treatment and affecting further response to the treatment, or a significant 'final' outcome" (p. 192).

The situation is oversimplified when only the learner's cognitive orientation is considered in planning the educational approach. However, we have begun with this single dimension with the belief that it will put us in a better position to extend the number of learner characteristics to include, for example, motivational and value orientation. We will describe this extension of the model in a later section.

Conception of the Environment (Educational Approaches)

The specification of an educational approach in matching model terms requires that the approach meet both criteria of theoretical adequacy and, at least to some extent, pedagogical reasonableness. The design must take into account various types of instruction and their relation to learner characteristics.

The generic dimension of the educational environment in the CL matching model is *degree of structure*, which is similar to what Schroder et al. (1967) refer to as environmental complexity. Degree of structure may take the form of variations in rule-example sequencing; example-only would be regarded as low structure while rule-example would be regarded as high structure. It may also be represented by variations from the low structure of a discovery approach to the high structure of a lecture approach; from independent to highly organized study, and from student-centered to teacher-centered approaches.

This use of multiple referents for the degree of structure is similar to Schroder et al.'s definition of environmental complexity. They used information load, informational diversity, rate of information change, noxity (amount of punishment) and eucity (amount of reward) as multiple referents for environmental complexity. The grouping of such approaches as discovery learning, example-first order in rule-example presentation, and student-centered approaches, because of their low degree of structure, does provide generality, but it also may neglect important differences. Therefore, it is important to re-evaluate the general definition continually.

Conception of the Interactive Process (Theory of Instruction)

Learner CL characteristics determine the basic matching predictions. In specifying predictions at this initial phase, we consider two points on the CL dimension: low CL, defined as scores in the range from 1.0 to 1.4, and high CL, defined as scores ranging above 1.8. Students lower in CL (below 1.0) are not presently considered because relatively few such students are encountered in the secondary schools where we are working. Similarly, students with scores from 1.4 to 1.8 are not included in the extreme group designs.

Given the characteristics of low CL learners (categorical, dependent on external standards, and incapable of generating their own concepts), one predicts that they will profit more from highly structured approaches. Given the characteristics of high CL learners (capable of generating new concepts, having a greater degree of internal standards, and being capable of taking on different perspectives), either they should profit more from low structured approaches or be unaffected by the degree of structure. Thus, the heart of the CL matching model is a generally inverse relation between CL and degree of structure: *Low CL learners profiting more from high structure and high CL learners profiting more from low structure, or in some cases, being less affected by variations in structure.*

Snow (1969) suggested two models for thinking about ATI hypotheses which are pertinent to the matching model here. His models (which are not necessarily mutually exclusive) are a compensatory model and a preferential model. He described the compensatory model as follows:

"Here we might argue that the treatments should compensate for each learner's deficiency by providing the mode of representation that the learner cannot provide for himself" (p. 15).

"The preceding discussions lead toward a general conception of instructional treatments as prosthetic devices for particular aptitude groups. A treatment that proves especially appropriate for a person deficient in some particular aptitude may be functioning as an 'artificial' aptitude. It contains the information processing functions that the learner cannot provide for himself" (p. 21).

The hypothesized relation between low CL learners and high structure is clearly an example of the compensatory model. Perhaps the reason for the ambiguity of prediction for high CL learners (either profit from low structure or are unaffected) can be understood by considering Snow's preferential model in which "The treatments are designed to capitalize on the apparent strengths and preferences of each kind of learner" (p. 15).

If only compensatory factors were at work, then one would expect only ordinal interactions between CL and variations in structure. High CL learners would do well under both conditions, while low CL learners would do well only under high structure (see Figure 2 for an example). However, the compensatory model provides no basis for understanding the occurrence of disordinal, or crossover interactions.

Why should a high CL learner perform more poorly than a low CL learner in a treatment, when he presumably has the requisite information processing capacities for better performance? (See Figure 3 for a qualified example.) One possible answer comes from Snow's preferential model. On this basis, one would understand the high CL decrement in performance as reflecting interference with the learner's preference or attitude. Thus the high CL learner with a capacity for generating his own solutions might resent a high structure treatment, and his performance might deteriorate accordingly.

It should be clear that we do not regard the compensatory and preferential models as providing highly precise means for deriving hypotheses; rather, they are provisional ways of thinking about person-environment interactions. In the discussion of empirical evidence for the CL matching model, it will be noted that in some cases we expected disordinal interactions and, in other cases, we hedged the

44

prediction for high CL learners because we did not know to what extent preferential factors would operate.

Specific Tasks (Subject Matter)

It would be naive to conclude without at least mentioning the issue of task specificity, the role of skill level, and its relation to content. Without minimizing the importance of the relation between learner skill level and content, we have thus far designed novel materials and tasks for the matching studies in order to minimize this factor. As we proceed, it is unquestionably necessary to coordinate elements of subject matter into the definition of degree of structure.

EMPIRICAL SUPPORT FOR CONCEPTUAL LEVEL MATCHING MODEL

The Upward Bound evaluation results described in Chapter I and the results of the homogeneous grouping study described in Chapter II both supported the CL matching model. In addition, several studies have been conducted more recently.

Using a matching model, McLachlan (1969) investigated the interactive effects of learner CL and variations in structure. These variations were represented by a discovery (low structure) vs. lecture (high structure) approach. Equal numbers of low and high CL students, matched on ability, were assigned to each of the two conditions. The content of the presentation consisted of a specifically designed set of visual materials aimed at acquainting the student with the Picasso painting, *Guernica*. Students in both conditions were shown the same pictorial materials, a slide containing the entire picture and a series of component parts of the picture on separate slides. Students in the lecture condition heard a short lecturette on the meaning of each component slide; while students in the discovery condition viewed each slide for a comparable amount of time, but were instructed to work out for themselves what the picture meant. Afterward, students were asked to give their own idea of the central meaning of the picture, and how the parts fitted together into this meaning (subjective integration). In addition, measures of recall and attitude were recorded. Figure 2 indicates the pattern of results for subjective integration.

Results indicated an ordinal interaction, with the low CL students performing significantly better ($p < .05$) with high structure (lecture) than with low structure (discovery). Since no differences were noted for the high CL students, this pattern illustrates the compensatory model suggested by Snow.

In a companion study, Tomlinson (1969) used the matching model rationale to investigate the differential effects of rule-example order as a function of learner CL. Groups of low and high CL students were assigned equally to three treatment conditions varying in degree of structure. Low structure consisted of instruction by first presenting the examples, with the rule presented at a much later time. Intermediate structure consisted of instructions in which the examples were presented first followed almost immediately by the rule. In the high structure condition, the rule was presented before the examples. The rule, or principle, was Festinger's (1957) concept of "cognitive dissonance," and the examples were included in a brief excerpt from a story about two college boys. Students' concept learning was

45

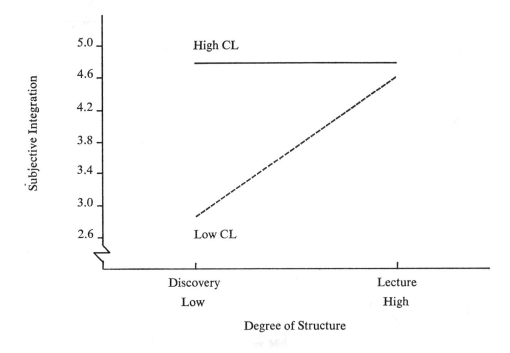

Figure 2 / Subjective Integration as a Function of Discovery vs. Lecture and Learner CL

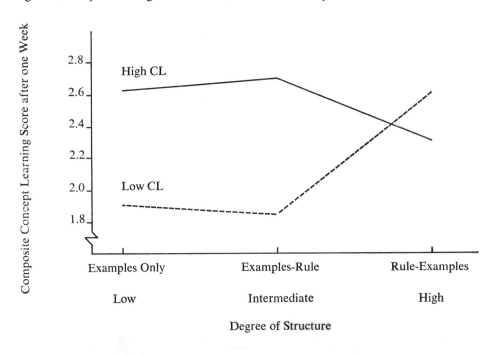

Figure 3 / Concept Learning as a Function of Rule-Example Order and Learner CL

indexed by multiple criteria: definition of concept, recall of examples, and production of new examples. Figure 3 presents the composite scores recorded one week after instruction.

Analysis of the results in Figure 3 indicated a highly significant CL x treatment effect (IQ effects having been removed by regression), and the expected pattern was borne out when comparing the mean scores. Under conditions of low and intermediate structure, the low CL groups were significantly lower ($p < .05$) than the high CL groups. The low CL groups under low and intermediate structure were also significantly lower ($p < .05$) than the low CL group under high structure. Although there was a tendency toward disordinal interaction, the difference between CL groups in the high structure condition was not significant. Nonetheless, this tendency toward a high CL "decrement" illustrates the principle in the preferential model suggested by Snow.

Finally, a study by Tuckman (1968) should be noted even though he used an objective test (Interpersonal Topical Inventory) for indexing CL rather than the paragraph completion method. He investigated the interactive effects of learner CL with degree of structure, in this case represented by non-directive teachers (low structure) vs. directive teachers (high structure). He followed the CL matching model rationale to predict matching effects for low CL students with directive teachers and for high CL students with non-directive teachers. When the measures of teacher preference, satisfaction, and course grade were analyzed, he found that the primary effects occurred in one mismatched cell. Compared to the other three combinations, the high CL students with directive teachers rated these teachers lower, and were less satisfied with them, thus providing an even clearer illustration of Snow's preferential model.

EXTENSION OF THE MODEL: ACCESSIBILITY CHANNELS

Although the results we have reviewed in relation to the CL matching model are encouraging, it is also obvious that other learner characteristics need to be considered. The model has therefore been extended to include other possible person-environment combinations, and in this extended model, the student is viewed in terms of accessibility channels.

Taking account of accessibility channels is almost unavoidable when working with a physically handicapped student. Though its need is less apparent for normal students, it seems equally important to consider them in terms of channels of accessibility so that the form of educational approach can be most appropriately tuned in to each student. The CL matching model gives an example of how the accessibility channel, learner's cognitive orientation, can be used to tune in, by modulating the structure of the presentation. The model in Table 6 extends this rationale to other orientations. Table 6 deals only with the coordination between the form of educational approach and the accessibility channel, and is not concerned with the relation between learner's skill level and the content of the presentation.

Table 6 presents the general nature of the relation, but in order to be useful for designing investigations or contributing to educational decisions, these general

Table 6 / Model for Coordinating Learner Characteristics with Educational Approaches

Accessibility channels	Form of presentation
1. Cognitive orientation	Structure of presentation
2. Motivational orientation	Form of feedback and reward
3. Value orientation	Value context of presentation
4. Sensory orientation	Modality of presentation

relations must be translated into more specific forms, comparable to the low CL-high structure prescription in the CL matching model. When matching motivational orientation with form of feedback and reward, the hypothesis would be that learners with self-directed orientations are more likely to profit from intrinsic reward and self-anchored feedback; while learners with more socially based orientation are more likely to profit from extrinsic reward and normative feedback. When matching value orientation with value content of the presentation, the central hypothesis would be that these learners are more likely to profit from a presentation within the "latitude of acceptance" of their current value orientation, and less likely to profit from a presentation either identical to their present stand, or outside their latitude of acceptance. Finally, when matching sensory orientation and modality of presentation, the obvious hypothesis is that when learners have a preferred modality, such as visual or auditory, they will profit more from a presentation in that modality. The rationale for these matching hypotheses will be amplified in Chapter V.

Investigations are planned that will attempt not only to test these hypotheses as we have done with the CL matching model, but also to consider the possible role of more than one accessibility channel in response to a treatment variation. Table 6 provides the basis of investigations to determine whether, for example, CL is more important than motivational orientation in determining differential response to structure of presentation. Conversely, does motivational orientation provide a better differential predictor of reaction to form of feedback and reward than cognitive orientation? Since we have reported only positive evidence, it should be noted that there is some evidence that bears on this last question, but not as predicted in the Table 6 model. Stuempfig and Maehr (1970) reported differential CL effects upon reaction to personal or impersonal feedback: while high CL students showed no variation between feedback conditions, low CL students performed better with personal rather than impersonal feedback. (No measure of motivational orientation was available.) Therefore, there is clearly a need to circumscribe those areas in which CL will provide differential reactions and those conditions that will be susceptible to other orientations. Table 6 should serve as a useful guide in collecting such information.

As the proposed accessibility channels are found to be functionally related to students' differential susceptibility to different educational approaches, the results of such research can have important implications for the school psychologist. He is often accused of gathering information about students that has nothing to do with the decisions teachers and educational planners must make. The model in Table 6 suggests that if the school psychologist could provide a profile of a student in terms of accessibility channels, such information might be quite helpful.

Finally, there is an obvious comment regarding construct validity of personality measures. Although its importance has frequently been implied, the degree to which a personality construct will predict differential response to different forms of environmental effect has not received sufficient emphasis. Although there can be a danger in limiting ourselves to pragmatic criteria, it seems worthwhile to suggest that when a measure of personality is described, one of the most valuable bits of information is the degree to which a person's variation on the measure gives some prediction of his differential reaction to different environmental effects.

PROBLEMS OF IMPLEMENTATION

Having described CL and summarized its construct validity, derived the rationale for the CL matching model and provided some evidence of its construct validity, and indicated some directions for extending it, we are left with the question of what effect these principles can and should have on educational practice.

Of course, the prime consideration is whether the principle is sufficiently well established to attempt implementation, and such proof of validity should not be ignored. However, at the risk of seeming cynical, it seems unlikely to me that the validity of an educationally-relevant psychological principle will have much to do with its acceptance in educational practice. Validity of a principle is probably a necessary, but certainly not a sufficient, condition to insure its adoption.

Assuming that the matching principle is sufficiently well established, it seems probable that one of the major determinants of its acceptability will be the degree to which it is congruent with the teacher's own ideas of matching. If so, then the task of implementing a matching model should begin with an investigation of what implicit matching model the educational decision-maker is now using. From what we know of attitude change and adoption of new procedures, the proposed matching prescriptions should not be too far out of line with those held by the person implementing them. Such problems of implementation will require concepts and strategies at least as comprehensive as those set forth in this book on matching.

One final complicating feature in the possible adoption of matching principles in the schools is the increasing tendency toward student-determined options and courses. How does a matching model operate in a situation where the students themselves decide the prescriptions? Ways must be explored to provide matching information to students in a constructive, non-threatening manner so that it can help them arrive at effective decisions themselves.

The first three chapters have discussed matching educational environments to *students*. The remaining chapters will discuss matching principles for the training of *teachers*. To provide the variety of environments called for in matching prescriptions requires highly skilled teachers. Chapter IV analyzes the skills required by teachers (and other training agents) who apply differential procedures. It then suggests the implications of the skill analysis model for planning training programs. Like the model in Chapter II, this model is an early statement. It will be extended in Chapter V.

CHAPTER IV

A Model for Analyzing the Training of Training Agents

Education, psychotherapy, social case work, and child-rearing are typically considered separately rather than together. However, a teacher, a psychotherapist, a social worker, and a parent share at least one common feature: they each provide an interpersonal *environment* for the person or group with whom they interact. To emphasize this generic similarity, we have described such persons as *training agents*. Use of this term enables us to coordinate some of the many environmental conditions which a child encounters in the home, school, and clinic.

Up to now we have been considering how the environments radiated by training agents affect the course of a person's development or learning. Now we analyze how these training agents learn to radiate appropriate environments. A better understanding of how to prepare training agents should facilitate the implementation of the matching models in Chapter II and III, since these models require that an agent be capable of radiating specific environments. A model for analyzing the training of training agents is also potentially valuable for illuminating the general training of professional workers (whom we will refer to as *trainees*). The aim of training procedures is typically to enable the trainee to become better able to radiate environments which will induce certain changes in a person or group. Therefore, the model is primarily applicable to the training of professional workers, teachers, psychotherapists, social workers, and probation officers, but there is no reason that it could not be applied to the training or re-education of parents (cf. Brim, 1959).

Questions in the training of professional workers abound. Under what conditions is learning by imitation most effective? Is awareness of one's role as an environmental influence necessary? Under what conditions is role playing valuable?

51

What is the appropriate pacing of intellectual understanding and direct experience? Is direct feedback more valuable early in training, or later, after forming categories within which the feedback can be processed? What is the most appropriate synchronization between the learning of specific environmental tactics and the learning of long-term strategy?

Before these questions can be answered, the job for which the trainee is being prepared must be described. Therefore, we will set forth a specific job description of a training agent, and specify the components of agent effectiveness in operational terms, much as an industrial psychologist might analyze the job of a factory worker. Such descriptions are essential for planning a training program and evaluating its effectiveness.

Following the form of models described in earlier chapters, we specify the objectives or desired state by defining agent effectiveness. Next, we describe the specific skills a trainee needs to accomplish this objective. Then we describe procedures most likely to facilitate the trainee's learning these skills, and methods of assessing them. The training model is similar in form to the Conceptual Systems model in Chapter II which analyzed the process of personality development. It specified the desired state of high Conceptual Level, set forth the stages of conceptual development through which progress toward this state occurred, and finally prescribed environmental conditions most likely to produce such progression. Here we use those specific environments prescribed in the student matching models as examples of environments to be learned by trainees. (The training model should also be applicable to learning environments outside the Conceptual Level theoretical domain.) The training model differs from the student model in that the procedures proposed here for teaching skills, and the hierarchical order of skill components are set forth, as areas to be investigated rather than as theoretically derived assertions.

THE DESIRED STATE: AGENT EFFECTIVENESS

Agent effectiveness is presently defined as the capacity to radiate a wide variety of environments, to select from this variety a specific environment to be radiated toward a particular person or group (with the aim of producing a particular behavioral outcome), and to shift from one environment to another under appropriate circumstances. Teacher effectiveness is defined as the capacity to present the same lesson in a variety of instructional forms (environments), to select and use that form most appropriate to produce a desired outcome with a particular group of students, and to shift to a new form when necessary. In a similar way, the effectiveness of a social worker is defined in terms of his capacity to relate to a client in a variety of environmental forms, to use the form of treatment most likely to produce a particular outcome with a specific kind of client, and to shift to a different treatment stance when necessary.

Kurt Lewin's formula, $B = f(P,E)$, or (Behavior is a function of the Person and the Environment) has been considered in the context of providing the appropriate environment (E) for the person (P) (Chapter III). It is a useful way to conceptualize differential treatment or intervention from the viewpoint of the developing child, the student or client. Now let us consider this formula from the standpoint of the training agent who controls only one factor in this relationship, the Environment. Let us restate it to read E: P→B (Environment radiated toward a Person leads to Behavior). The effective agent specifies a desired behavior (B) for a person (P) and then selects from his repertory of environments that specific one (E) most likely to produce the desired result. A teacher wishing to induce critical thinking (B_1) from an inquisitive child (P_I), for example, might select and radiate a reflective environment (E_x) in order to produce this result.

To perform such complex activity successfully requires many skills. The agent must have a variety of environments in his skill battery, and be able to select the most appropriate one in each case. To do this he must understand the differential use of environments in relation to long-term objectives, and to the intermediate steps toward these objectives. Agent effectiveness therefore includes both his ability to use differential approaches, or radiate specific environments, and his understanding of when to utilize a specific environment or shift to another. Professional schools differ considerably in the order of teaching skill and knowledge to trainees. Whether theory should precede, accompany, or follow specific skill acquisition is an empirical question which needs exploration.

In order to explore such problems we need to specify the components underlying agent effectiveness which are summarized in Table 7. We use the three factors in the relationship – Environments, Behaviors, and Persons – as the basic units in describing the components underlying agent effectiveness.

The table shows the pattern to be followed in this chapter as we discuss each of these skills in turn. After describing the skill, we suggest methods of assessment

Table 7 / Training Objectives

Objective	Definition of Objective		
Skill in discrimination	To discriminate between environments	To discriminate between behaviors	To discriminate between persons
	E_x / E_y / E_z	B_1 / B_2 / B_3	P_I / P_{II} / P_{III}
Skill in radiating environments	To radiate a variety of environments	To radiate that environment which will produce a specific behavior	To radiate that environment which will produce a specific behavior from a particular person
	E_x: E_y: E_z:	E_x: → B_1 E_y: → B_2	E_x: P_I → B_1 E_y: P_{II} → B_1
Skill in flexible modulation from one environment to another		To shift from one environment to another under appropriate circumstances	
		(Time 1) E_x: P_I → B_1 (Time 2) E_y: P_I → B_3	

Code: E = Environment   B = Behavior   P = Person

and procedures for training. We will present the skills in a general order from the more simple to the more complex, but the optimal sequence to be employed in the actual training of such skill acquisition remains an empirical question.

SKILL IN DISCRIMINATION

To Discriminate between Environments ($E_x/E_y/E_z$)

Before a trainee can learn to radiate a variety of environments, he must be aware of the differences between these environments and be capable of accurately classifying them. For example, consider the following teacher comments, which may be viewed as environmental stimuli to be classified:

"I'm disappointed in you."

"That's right."

"That's interesting – any other ideas?"

"How could you go about checking on your ideas?"

The first two teacher comments might be classified together as representing teacher-centered reactions, and are somewhat different from the last two, which might be classified as being reflective or student-centered.

A basic discrimination to be learned by psychotherapy trainees is between directive and nondirective therapeutic environments. From the present viewpoint, the trainee's learning to make this discrimination, and learning to classify therapist comments into one of these two categories is an essential skill, regardless of which therapeutic environment the trainee may ultimately utilize. Implicit in the present approach is the belief that the controversies between directive and nondirective therapies are not very fruitful because a well trained psychotherapist should be capable of radiating either therapeutic environment and seeing its utility in different contexts.

To Discriminate between Behaviors ($B_1/B_2/B_3$)

The trainee needs to be capable of discriminating accurately between the various behavioral outcomes he will encounter. The domain of behaviors to be discriminated will obviously be those responses made by persons with whom the trainee works, so the domain of behaviors will vary from teacher to social worker to psychotherapist. For example, a teacher trainee needs a taxonomy of student behavior to discriminate between different types of student behavior. Let us consider the following student responses as stimuli to be classified:

"The square root of 49 is 7."

"Hamlet is a tragedy written by Shakespeare."

"I have a hunch about the main character in this study."

"Maybe we should consider the effect of rainfall on the kind of house they build."

The teacher trainee may place the first and second together as assertions of fact, discriminating them from the last two categories which are hypotheses. Unless the teacher trainee can quickly and accurately classify student responses, he will not be in a position to evaluate the effect of the environment he radiates.

For a social worker the behavioral stimuli may be client remarks such as the following:

"It isn't my fault I got in trouble."

"No matter what I do, things still turn out the same."

"Maybe if I try this, then that might improve things."

"I can see where part of this may be my fault."

Here the social worker trainee is likely to classify the first two as negation or denial of responsibility and thus discriminate them from the last two which may be classified as acceptance of responsibility. The classification system will vary with the theoretical orientation, but the trainee's task is to learn to use whatever system of classification is appropriate in order to discriminate between client reactions and to classify them reliably. The trainee should be capable of classifying behavioral outcomes as rapidly as he sorts objects into classes according to their size or color.

To Discriminate between Persons ($P_I/P_{II}/P_{III}$)

In teacher training this skill might be included in the study of individual differences, or in understanding the child, while in psychotherapy training such skill acquisition might be considered diagnostic ability. Among the very large number of classification methods available, the most useful appear to be person characteristics directly related to differential reaction to environmental effects, as described in Chapter III. Does the differential discrimination of persons in the classification system carry with it a differential prescription of effective environments? If not, the classification of persons has little or no function. The system for classifying delinquent youths developed by Warren and her associates (1964), and described in Chapter I is a good example. Using this system, the training agent can translate the youth's classification on the interpersonal maturity scale to the most appropriate form of therapeutic intervention and most reasonable treatment goals. Such functional classification is in sharp contrast to the frequently dysfunctional utility of the Kraepelinian diagnostic classification system, which was developed in a static typological framework. Examples of classification systems for educational intervention were described in Chapters II and III.

The importance of sizing up the person with whom one communicates is nicely illustrated by Flavell (1968). He investigated children's discrimination of the other person's role, that is his disposition, capabilities, and limitations, in order to communicate more effectively with him. Using the stimulus variation of blindfolded as compared to sighted persons, Flavell found that skill in discrimination increased with age, that is, older children are more likely to vary or modulate the communication to fit the characteristics of the person.

Obviously, the trainee must learn to classify the person with whom he is working in some functional system. In person classification, skill is considered to be similar, but more complex than skill in classifying behaviors, since the person's behavior provides an important part of the discriminative classification. Social psychological investigations in person perception and impression formation provide methods for measuring how effectively a trainee can make discriminations between persons. A more complex component of skill in sizing up the persons with whom one works is the capacity to evoke cues from him which permit classification, and this skill may also need to be acquired.

55

Assessment of Discriminative Skill

The procedures for assessing how effectively a trainee can discriminate in each of these three areas are generally similar. The only difference lies in the stimuli presented: Behaviors, Environments, or Persons. In all three cases, the stimuli can be presented on paper (as in examples above), on tape, film, or hypothetically through role playing. Obviously, the more adequately the mode of presentation represents the actual Behavior, Environment, or Person, the more precise will be the measurement.

Response form of the method may vary also, from a free response (referring to questions like "Which ones go together? Why?") to requesting the trainee to classify according to predetermined categories. The free response form is similar to the discovery method in that the trainee must generate his own dimensions along which he will make discriminations, while the other is more structured.

Davitz (1964) has developed methods of assessing sensitivity to emotional expression. In one method, subjects were asked to listen to the same statement presented several times in different emotional contexts. Each subject was given a list of ten emotions and asked to associate one of them with each of the different statements. Assessment of discriminative skill was based on how well the subjects' judgements agreed with those of a large group of trained judges who had agreed on clasifications. Davitz followed a similar procedure using stimuli of drawings and musical sounds, illustrating the possible range in mode of presentation. Although his purpose was slightly different from the training model, the generic assessment approach is identical.

A method for assessing skill in discriminating environments is readily available, since several coding systems for classifying teacher behavior (e.g., Joyce & Harootunian, 1967) or therapist reaction have been devised. Thus one may simply use as stimuli pre-coded environmental events (teacher or therapist reaction) with instructions for the trainee to code these environmental occurrences according to the manual provided. Discriminative skill thus becomes identical to rater reliability in relation to some pre-established norm.

Kahn & Connell (1957) have developed an ingenious method for coding the environment radiated by an interviewer. In their approach, the trainee is requested to code the interviewer's reaction (environment in present terms) on three dimensions: acceptance (supports or rejects respondent), validity (unbiased or biased), and relevance (toward or away from desired objective). Although this approach involves a multidimensional classification of the stimuli, the classification is functionally related to later skill acquisition of the interviewer trainee.

If measures of each of these three discriminative skills are available, they serve several purposes. At the beginning of training, a base rate profile spotlights areas of deficiency in which training is needed. Conversely, if a trainee has a high skill level in one or more areas, then there is no particular value in exposing him to training to increase that specific skill. Thus, one purpose is to maximize training efficiency by discarding the traditional lock-step training program and substituting a more individually tailored program, designed according to the differential skill profile of each trainee. A second purpose is achieved if the measures are administered after train-

56

ing, so that some index of skill acquisition may be derived, and the differential effectiveness of various training procedures evaluated.

Procedures for Training Discriminative Skill

Much more is presently known about how to assess variation in discriminative skill than about what techniques are likely to increase the level of such skill. For example, after outlining in detail several methods for assessing emotional sensitivity, Davitz (1964) concludes his book stating that we need to learn more about "the development of effective training procedures to increase sensitivity" (p. 202).

Two approaches appear potentially valuable for suggesting procedures for increasing discriminative skill. The first is the area of traditional psychophysics in which considerable empirical knowledge is available regarding how the skill in discriminating physical objects can be acquired or increased. This literature should prove quite useful in providing leads regarding such factors as the optimal order of presentation and the importance of anchoring effects. The second approach is that of the sensitivity training employed in T-group training (Bradford, Gibb, & Benne, 1964) which deals directly with the enhancement of interpersonal discrimination. For the present we will simply suggest that these sources provide the basis upon which one may devise procedures for enhancing discriminative skill. Once the skill has been described objectively (as we have done in the previous sections) then experimentation may proceed toward evaluating which procedure will be most effective in enhancing it. Also implicit in our use of examples is the belief that a side benefit of viewing teacher trainee psychotherapy trainees, and social workers generically as trainees is the possibility of cross-stimulation between the professional schools in these various dicipline.

SKILL IN RADIATING ENVIRONMENTS

To Radiate a Variety of Environments (E_x: , E_y: , E_z:)

Once the trainee has learned to discriminate between environments radiated by others, he needs to learn to radiate those environments himself. Trainees initially vary considerably in their preferred environmental style, for example, their teaching style or therapeutic style, and it is important to measure this preferred style or styles at the beginning of training. Teacher trainees entering training may exhibit preferred styles ranging from directive to supportive to reflective. The trainee who is primarily supportive will therefore need to learn to radiate directive and reflective environments. Ideally he should be able to convey the same lesson topic through different environmental contexts when appropriate.

Skill in radiating a variety of environments is purely a performance skill, much like playing a role on command. We intentionally distinguish this performance skill, in which the trainee is instructed to radiate a specific environment, from the skill in which the trainee must size up the situation himself, come to some conclusion about the most effective environment, and then radiate it. The distinction seems useful because a trainee may fail at the more complex task, either because of his inability to size up the situation, or because of his inability to radiate the prescribed environment.

Although we are presently contending that capacity to radiate a wide variety of environments is an important skill component, it should be noted that certain rather specific jobs may require only a limited repertory of environments. In such cases it may be more efficient to *select* agents who already have available the requisite environmental skill as part of their preferred style than to attempt to produce such skill through training.

The preferred style of a teacher trainee just entering training is likely embedded in a value matrix of how learning occurs and what is the best way to induce such learning through teaching procedures (see Chapter V). For example, consider the following responses given by two trainees about to enter teacher training to the statement "The most important thing in teaching is":

> Trainee A: "Interest in subject matter and accomplishment in subject matter. If one is devoted to this, one can perhaps indirectly surmount the problem of personal relationships with the students."

> Trainee B: "To develop creativity and critical thinking. It is *not* the rote memorization of facts and formulas. I feel that creativity and critical thinking can be developed in the ordinary classroom situation if the teacher emphasizes them."

It seems quite clear that the preferred teaching styles which these trainees bring to the training situation will reflect these valued beliefs, and will probably be very different from each other. Therefore, in attempting to extend the trainee's environmental repertoire it is most important to present the environments in a non-value laden context as far as possible. The trainee should think about variations in environmental contexts much as he thinks about variation in media – TV, radio, newspapers – that is, as alternative, potentially interchangeable means of conveying information.

To Radiate that Environment which will Produce a Specified Behavior (E_x: → B)

Just as skill in radiating environments requires a capacity to discriminate between environments, so the manipulation of behavior by environmental control requires skill in radiating environments. In this component, the trainee is given the task of producing a specific behavior (from an unspecified person), and he must then radiate an environment which will produce this result. Obviously, this is a two-phase process. The new component involved here is the learning E: → B relations. In other words, he must learn what environment produces what behavior.

The trainee may learn E: → B relations in a mechanical "push-pull, click-click" fashion, or he may learn them as a part of a highly complex theoretical network. Since the behavior to be produced varies between trainees in education, therapy, and social work, the range of behaviors may be larger in some jobs than in others.

Ideally the trainee learns these E: → B relations as a number of causally related connections with a minimum of value judgment. If the trainee can, he may assimilate these E: → B relations through a process of intellectual curiosity. He might say, "I wonder what behavior results from a highly directive environment? Hmm . . . What do you know . . . that produces a reliable routine behavior pattern . . . that's

58

interesting!" This de-emphasis of value association is critical in early training because the trainee should later learn to see various environments and behavior as differentially valuable at certain phases in the learning or therapeutic process. The $E: \rightarrow B$ relations should be learned in a neutral way, much as one views a candy machine ("If I pull this I'll get a chocolate bar, and if I pull this I'll get a peanut cluster"). Then the trainee can later use these relations, as required, in a more objective fashion. (A later view on this issue is presented in Chapter V.)

The trainee can be asked to write down his assumption about what environment leads to what behavior before actually radiating the environment. Such a procedure involves what is usually called a lesson plan in teacher training, or a therapeutic strategy in therapy training.

To Radiate that Environment which will Produce a Specified Behavior from a Particular Person ($E_x : P_I \rightarrow B_1$)

In this skill, the trainee is given information about the behavior to be produced, and some information about the person; his job is to select and radiate that environment most likely to produce the desired result. This skill differs from the just discussed "push-pull" skill in that it must take into account the differential effectiveness of the environments on the person with whom one is working. We have intentionally placed this skill after the trainee has learned to radiate a variety of environments because variation in radiating environments is the one factor the trainee or agent has to control. He cannot usually control the kind of person with whom he works, but can modulate his environment to the characteristics of that person.

Some training programs begin with understanding the person, and feel that this person discrimination and individual modulation to persons should be given priority. In the present view, we hold that to give trainees a great deal of information about differential accessibility of persons when he has not yet been trained to use environments appropriate for these persons will simply lead to disappointment. He will sense the differences between the persons with whom he works, but be unable to do anything about it. However, as with many of the present assertions, the relative merits of these two sequences should be empirically evaluated.

Although it is probably possible to learn $E: \rightarrow B$ connections in a mechanical fashion, it seems less likely that trainees can acquire knowledge of them this way because they are so complex. Such learning should be embedded in a theoretical network which gives justification for the $E: P \rightarrow B$ relations, for example, the theoretical models in Chapters II and III.

Assessment of Skill in Radiating Environments

Although the three skills just described vary in complexity, the task of assessment has one common characteristic: the coding of the kind of environment which the trainee radiates. Once a reliable coding manual for classifying environments is available (e.g. Joyce & Harootunian, 1967), then this system can be used. Let us assume we wish to assess the variety of environments a trainee can radiate. For example, we might instruct a teacher trainee to teach a particular lesson (keeping content constant) in a structured environmental context, and then code the trainee's performance under these instructions. A similar procedure would then be followed for a

59

supportive environmental context, and a reflective environmental context. Each of these performance efforts would be coded to determine how closely the trainee radiated the prescribed environment. These presentations should also be analyzed to note how distinct one was from the other. During the training process, a trainee may have difficulty presenting two environments, say supportive and reflective, in distinctively different fashions. Such difficulty may represent some still remaining confusion in discriminating between these environments, or it may represent difficulty in extending cognitive discriminations to behavioral referents. In any case, an analysis of degree of distinctness will help.

It is clear from the assessment of incoming trainees that initial preferred style is significantly related to trainee Conceptual Level in that the high CL trainee is more likely to radiate a reflective environment as a preferred style (Hunt & Joyce, 1967). It is tempting to conclude from this relation that high CL trainees have more potential to radiate a variety of environments. While this may be so, it is sometimes as difficult to train high CL trainees to radiate a structured environment as it is to train low CL trainees to radiate a reflective environment. Again, we need to be cautious in prematurely imposing value judgements.

In assessing skill in E: → B, as well as producing specific behaviors, it will be useful to obtain an independent measure of the trainee's understanding and planning of the E: → B connection through a lesson plan or some other explication of intended strategy. The assessment of E: → B skill will likely take the form of a profile, in that certain trainees will be proficient in producing certain forms of behavior (either through proficiency in radiating the requisite environment, or in the ease with which they grasp the connection, or both), while they may be quite deficient in producing other forms of behavior. Thus, this assessment will depict a profile of skills over the relevant domain of E: → B possibilities.

Assessment of skill in the E: P → B realm becomes more complex and also necessarily more job-specific. If the trainee is to work entirely with withdrawn, mentally defective youngsters, then there is no reason for assessing (or training competence) in working with E: → B relations in which the person is a highly aggressive, acting out delinquent.

We have developed a prototype communication task for assessing such E: P → B skill (Hunt, 1970). The prototype task consisted simply of obtaining a fifteen minute behavior sample of the way in which the trainee communicated (conveyed through an environmental context) some information (in this case the concept of the balance of power in the U.S. Federal Government) to a specified person (a not too bright Venezuelan immigrant who hopes to become a U.S. citizen) with the behavioral purpose of increasing his understanding of the concept of checks and balances. Each trainee was given information on the topic, information about the person and the aim; and time to prepare a brief lesson plan or strategy. Finally he attempted to communicate this to a person who played the role of the Venezuelan. During the fifteen minute presentation, the role player systematically presented obstacles to effective communication, in the form of misunderstanding, impatience, erroneous understanding and the like. The trainee's behavior was coded along several dimensions to assess how effectively he took cognizance of the person's frame of reference and modulated ("flexed") to this frame of reference, and how effectively he dealt with various obstacles. We view this behavior sample as representing one E: P → B component which is important for almost all teachers. However, it is only one component. In order to obtain a representative picture of agent effectiveness, one needs to apply this assessment prototype to other E: P → B demands, a task which has been taken up by Weinstein (1965), who designed a task to determine how effectively a trainee can control and regulate a teaching situation.

Weinstein was interested in assessing applicants to be trained for teaching culturally deprived children. Experience in training such teachers has indicated that unless the trainee can establish a routine, and let the students know initially that he is in charge, that he will be in continual difficulty no matter how many other skills he may possess. Therefore, in this control task, the persons were three sixth grade students (role players) in a culturally deprived school. The desired behavior was to let them know the rules for the coming semester and to acquaint them with the teacher. The role players introduced systematic obstacles to the purpose of the trainee. The environment radiated by the trainee during the fifteen minute period was coded on relevant dimensions. This task illustrates the flexible possibilities for variations on the communication task prototype. We have also developed tasks in which the trainee must communicate the concept of scarcity to a concrete twelve-year-old, and one requiring the trainee to convey the idea of Thoreau's "Civil Disobedience" to three unruly adolescents. It is important to note that skill in the communication task is not necessarily highly correlated with skill in the control task. As we have suggested earlier such knowledge of relative strengths and weaknesses will provide the basis for pinpointing training resources.

Procedures for Training Skill in Radiating Environments

The specific question of how to induce a response which we have called "radiating an environment" can be viewed generally as the problem of how any response becomes acquired. From a theoretical view, this question is enormously complex; and from the practical side, since training institutions spend months and even years attempting to accomplish this goal, we can only touch on a few of the key issues, so that the differential effectiveness of various training procedures can then be empirically evaluated.

Campbell (1961) has distinguished six modes of response acquisition which can be applied to acquisition of skill in radiating environments:

"1. *Learning, blind trial-and-error, or locomotor exploration.*
2. *Perception.*
3. *Perceptual observation of the outcomes of another person's trial-and-error exploration.*
4. *Perceptual observation of another person's responses.*
5. *Linguistic instruction about the characteristics of objects.*
6. *Linguistic instruction about responses to be made"* (pp. 103-106).

Let us consider these procedures in relation to a trainee's attempt to acquire the response skill of radiating a reflective environment. The first two procedures are probably used least frequently in most current training programs. Learning to radiate a reflective environment only through the trial-and-error method, for example, would presumably also involve some differential reinforcement, so that the trainee's random efforts to radiate the "correct" environment would be gradually shaped. As Bandura (1965) observed, the use of shaping responses is highly inefficient when one is attempting to induce complex patterns of response, such as driving a car. The third and fourth procedures represent reliance on modeling and imitation. In training terms, these procedures consist of the teacher trainee's watching another trainee make mistakes (third procedure), or observing an experienced teacher (fourth procedure). Watching films or listening to tape recordings of other persons radiating environments are also examples of this type. The person observed may give a deliberately good or bad performance depending on the purpose of the illustration. The fifth and sixth procedures represent the more symbolic modes of response induction, in which the trainee is acquainted with the response pattern through verbal description. Most training procedures rely on a combination of these various techniques; they begin with linguistic instructions, then use perceptual observations of another person's responses and finally use learning. However, this taxonomy of procedures is helpful in analyzing various forms of training.

The response of radiating a specific environment is more difficult than the responses which Campbell described. Therefore, the trainee will need to spend considerable time attempting to execute the response pattern and profiting from his own mistakes through some confrontation with his performance. For example, there are procedures which confront the trainee with his own performance either through films (video feedback), or through tape recordings. We believe that the usefulness of these procedures depends in large part upon how well the trainee has learned to discriminate between environments. For a therapy trainee to profit from viewing or listening to his efforts at radiating environments toward a patient, he needs some system of coding his own environmental radiating, in order to evaluate it and if necessary make appropriate modifications. This belief could be put to an empirical test by simply observing two groups of trainees who receive video feedback training. One group would be trained in discriminative skill in classifying environments, and the other group would not. We would predict that the former group would profit more from the feedback experience than the latter.

Training for skill in $E: \rightarrow B$ is somewhat more complex. Procedures vary from mechanical push-pull to a highly theoretical conception of the human organism and its relation to environmental pressures. For most readers, the suggestion that trainees may acquire $E: \rightarrow B$ skill through a mechanical notion of how an environment produces a behavior is likely to be seen as impractical and perhaps non-humanistic. We would contend that these procedures deserve a try, mainly because many trainees are incapable of learning enough about the complexities of personality organization to understand thoroughly why certain $E: \rightarrow B$ combinations occur.

One intermediate procedure for training $E: \rightarrow B$ was used in a pilot study by Hunt, Joyce, & DelPopolo (1964). It involved generating hunches encouraged by a reflective environment. In this investigation, a small group of teacher trainees were seen in a brief workshop. The teacher trainees took the role of students while one of the investigators taught three brief lessons in each of three areas: mathematics, social studies, and English. The teacher intentionally radiated a highly reflective environment in all three lessons, during which the students were encouraged to generate hunches about the material in the lessons.

After each lesson, the teacher trainees discussed their own experiences and feelings during the lesson. They were encouraged to verbalize how they felt, for example, "I was afraid I would make a fool of myself if I said that" or "One of my ideas seemed so silly," and also to describe how the environment which they encountered fostered their bringing their hunches out in the open despite these reservations. During this discussion, the teacher trainees also discussed how they might have reacted if the environment had been very directive, and why they would not have felt comfortable in bringing out new hunches in such an atmosphere. Although the results of this pilot investigation were inconclusive, the general approach illustrates one possible method by which the trainee becomes aware of the $E: \to B$ connection through his own experience, and later verbalization of the process which he experienced.

As we have indicated in the examples in this section, many of the questions to be answered in relation to the most effective training procedures are concerned with the sequence of procedures rather than with the procedures themselves. For example, there is little question that a trainee who is aware of $E: \to B$ relations is more likely to be capable of radiating differential environments to produce differentially specified behaviors than a trainee who is unaware of such relations; but this does not necessarily mean that the process of arriving at such skill involves a training sequence in which he first learns to be aware of such relations. It is possible that the training procedure in which he first learns to execute the performance of a particular environment, and note its behavioral effects, without any understanding of the basis for the relation may be more effective.

Procedures for training $E: P \to B$ relations are likely to be even more complex and, as implied earlier, it seems less likely that such relations can be learned in a mechanical fashion. If the trainee has learned several $E: \to B$ relations for people in general, it may be that something similar to a cognitive conflict training procedure may be used. The trainee might be confronted by a person (or small number of persons, perhaps in a micro-teaching situation) for whom a particular $E: \to B$ relation does not work. After the trainee has used the particular environment which was supposed to produce the desired behavior, and finds it unsuccessful, he can then attempt to puzzle out why this environment did not work for this person or group.

For a trainee to learn $E: P \to B$ skill, he must become aware of how earlier learned distinctions between persons have relevance for differential reaction. We have found in in-service teacher training procedures that discussing differences between students in terms of the accessibility channels described in Chapter III is quite helpful. Once the trainee can radiate different environments, it seems likely that the most effective means for him to learn $E: P \to B$ relations is through some grasp of a theoretical model which provides a conceptual basis for these complex relations.

SKILL IN FLEXIBLE MODULATION FROM ONE ENVIRONMENT TO ANOTHER

Up to this point the skills discussed have been aimed at producing specific behaviors, with no attention to the sequential relation between behaviors over a period of time.

For example, a teacher with a group of culturally disadvantaged students whose personality orientation is predominantly Sub I, must initially radiate an environment which is highly structured, somewhat controlling, and also accepting. However, if the teacher is capable only of radiating strength and power in establishing initial structure, and is incapable of modulating to other more effective environments once the routine has been established, he is unlikely to be very effective. (Conversely, of course, the teacher who cannot initially radiate control in order to establish a line of march will also be ineffective but for very different reasons.)

In order to acquire skill in flexible modulation (or what we have called "flexing"), the trainee needs to acquire some temporal perspective. In education this may be a developmental perspective while in psychotherapy it may be a therapeutic perspective. In discussing this question, Lippitt, Watson, & Westley (1958) put the issue as follows: "We suggest again that no change agent can control the dynamic process of change unless he knows what has happened and what is happening. The techniques which enable him to find out what has happened and what is happening are therefore exceedingly important" (p. 289).

Some training agents can learn E: P→B relations for a particular group quite effectively, but are incapable of flexible modulation. In Chapter II we described some teachers who could learn the "recipe" that Stage I students were initially receptive to consistent environment with some competition. Such teachers began to use procedures, like debates, which are functionally good for these students. But although such environments helped Stage I students function better, they could ultimately produce arrestation if not modulated. Therefore, we attempted to convey the notion that although debates, for example, may be initially effective for Stage I students, the teacher should gradually introduce an environment to foster student distinctions within the pro versus con dichotomy of debates. In this way the students could learn to appreciate distinctions in the viewpoints of students who were all on one side of a particular issue. Only when he is encouraged to make such distinctions can the Stage I student begin to develop independence.

It is essential for trainees to learn this distinction between functional and developmental goals, and the environments to produce them. Learning to modulate to another environment, once one behavior has been evoked, probably occurs most effectively when the trainee is provided with some theory of how these behaviors combine in the course of continuous development.

Flexible modulation of environments may be called for within a single lesson or therapeutic session, it may be called for in dealing with heterogeneous groups, where there is a differential receptivity of persons to environments, or it may be called for in the long-term planning of strategy for change. In any case, there seems to be reason to believe that flexible modulation cannot occur unless the trainee has the three sub-skills described in the preceding section.

Skill in flexible modulation also requires the explication of the desired behavioral or organizational changes which the training agent is attempting to produce, by the goals of education, or of therapy. If the accepted goal of education is simply to increase scores on objective achievement examinations, this limited goal may not be fostered by encouraging conceptual development since we know (Chapter II) that Stage I students score higher on objective examinations than do Stage II students.

64

However, if we want more critical thinking and creativity, then environments which will facilitate conceptual progression are appropriate. Put another way, when one analyzes the role of the training agent in terms of flexible modulation, then it becomes critical to establish the desired behaviors toward which such modulation is aimed. Thus, the present explication of the training process cannot proceed effectively unless one has also explicitly acknowledged the goals of the change process within which the training agent is working.

Assessment of capacity to modulate flexibly is conducted with procedures similar to those described in the previous section. However, in this case the person with whom the trainee is working (the role player) must change his behavior systematically, in order to observe how effectively the trainee can "flex" in relation to such changes.

We have presented a model for analyzing the training of training agents which is applicable to the assessment, training, and placement of teachers, psychotherapists, social workers, and other training agents whose function is to provide an interpersonal environment. Training agent effectiveness was defined as the capacity to radiate a wide variety of environments; to select from this variety a specific environment to be radiated toward a particular person or group, with the aim of producing a particular behavioral outcome; and to shift from one environment to another under appropriate circumstances. Using a variation of the Lewinian $B = f(P,E)$ formula, we considered the job of the training agent in terms of $E: P \rightarrow B$ (or the environment directed toward a person produces a behavior). Skill components underlying agent effectiveness – discriminative skill, skill in radiating environments, and capacity to shift from one environment to another – are described; techniques for assessing such skill are considered; and procedures for training these skills discussed.

If the present definition of agent effectiveness is accepted, this model provides the basis for designing investigations to learn more about how such skills can be acquired most effectively. The assessment of trainees in terms of differential skills should also provide a means for making training procedures more efficient. Finally, it hoped that viewing teachers, therapists, and social workers as generically similar has the potential advantage of increasing knowledge about training procedures through interprofessional cross-stimulation.

CHAPTER V

Matching Models for Teacher Training

The training of teachers, like the education of children, requires adaptation to individual differences. Teacher trainees vary enormously in skill level and in personality, yet most programs for training teachers are designed for an average trainee, with few options to accommodate trainee variation. A teacher training program, which provides alternative experiences modulated to trainee differences, is not only more likely to produce an efficient direct effect, but it will also be indirectly beneficial in providing the teacher trainee with an experimental example of what is meant by individualizing instruction and "meeting the needs of the student."

In teacher training, adaptation to individual differences requires a system for coordinating differences in educational environments (or training intervention) with trainee characteristics. We will use the concept of matching to describe the appropriateness of a particular training intervention, for an individual trainee, to accomplish a specific training objective. Matching has been used in earlier chapters to describe situations in which the teacher himself radiates an environment toward a student, for example, a teacher presents a didactic lesson which is either matched or mis-matched to a student, given certain objectives. However, analysis in terms of matching should be equally useful here, and requires only that we use the term, *training intervention*, to make clear that the environment in differential teacher training refers to intervention procedures directed toward the teacher trainee, as distinct from those environments which he will learn to radiate later toward students.

Matching models for teacher training should provide the basis for coordinating trainee characteristics, such as skill level and aptitudes, with variations in training intervention. Trainee skill level will determine the specific content of the training

67

intervention, while the trainee's aptitudes, or accessibility characteristics (described in Chapter III), will determine the form of the training intervention. A matching model in training states two knowns – the immediate training objective and the relevant trainee characteristics – and prescribes the third: a specific training intervention. Matching models are based on the assumption that different people learn different things in different ways; thus, the planning and design of any educational program, including the training of teachers, should provide differential alternatives toward the same or different goals. The notion that there is no single best program for training teachers is fundamental to this view. The reader is likely to nod in agreement with this belief, as he might agree with the importance of "meeting the needs of each child." However, if one intends only to give lip service to the idea of adapting training to individual differences of trainees, then the specific prescriptions outlined here will serve little purpose.

Several assumptions underlie this differential training approach. First, that the design and planning of a training program must begin with a thorough understanding of the variation in trainees who will attend; it is not developed according to general specifications, ignoring trainee characteristics. Second, that there will be sufficient variation among trainees to warrant adapting training intervention to such trainee differences. Third, regardless of the amount of variation among the trainees, that a careful analysis of the "match" between trainee and intervention is likely to force a more explicit analysis of the process involved in how trainees change during training.

In what follows, this analysis consists of: stating certain training objectives; considering certain trainee characteristics relevant to intervention; specifying related aspects of training intervention; and finally, deriving those trainee-intervention combinations most likely to produce the desired objectives.

THE MATCHING MODELS

Training Objectives

The training of teachers is considered one example of the training of training agents. As used in Chapter IV, the term, training agent describes a person who provides an interpersonal environment (E), for the person or group (P), with whom he interacts, to produce a particular behavioral effect or change (B). Therefore, although the model will be described specifically for the training of teachers, it should also apply to the training of other training agents: psychotherapists, counselors, social workers, industrial trainees, and even parents.

One of the most useful forms for specifying objectives is to state them in terms of components characterizing the effective training agent. Component analysis permits initial characterization of a trainee in terms of a component profile, and subsequent evaluation of various forms of intervention, by noting the degree of component change produced. For example, we have used three components – adaptability, motivational orientation, and interpersonal competence – to assess trainees (Hunt, 1965b), and to suggest how different component profiles might be required for different assignments. Harrison and Oshry (1967) have developed an Organizational Behavior Describer Survey for use in industry, which consists of four components: rational and technical competence, verbal dominance, emotional expressiveness, and consideration. In the area of psychotherapist and counselor effectiveness, Truax and Carkhuff (1967) have suggested three essential components: empathy, non-expressive warmth, and genuineness. More specifically relevant to the training of teachers are the components suggested by Joyce (1969): making and using knowledge, shaping the school, teaching with strategy, creating interpersonal climates, and controlling the self. Teacher sensitivity (the capacity to react appropriately to the learner's frame of reference) and teacher strength (the capacity to structure and organize the classroom) have also been used as two components useful in assessing and planning for differential treatment of teacher trainees (Hunt, 1970).

Another system of component analysis is that described in Chapter IV: skill in discrimination, skill in radiating environments, and skill in flexible modulation from one environment to another.

When training objectives are expressed in terms of components, they can be operationally defined, permitting an assessment of each trainee's present position on a component profile. An inspection of the trainee's component profile indicates those areas in which further training is required. In order for a component system to serve as the basis for planning a training program, some understanding of the relations between the components is required. If a trainee is deficient in several components, then the first practical issue is to decide on which component he should first receive training, a decision which requires consideration of the order and sequence of components. In the model summarized in Table 7, it was assumed that the three sub-components in discriminative skill — discriminating between environments, discriminating between behaviors, and discriminating between persons — were prerequisites for skill in radiating an environment to produce a specific behavior; some recent research, conducted in a different conceptual context (Brooks, 1967), supports this assumption.

Order of intervention may also be determined by the potential ease or difficulty of inducing change in a component, since it may be advisable to begin with a component on which change is more likely to occur. Also, there is the question of how many of the components can realistically be expected to change in the training time available. If planners are willing to settle for a circumscribed set of component skills, then, of course, this will affect strategy in specifying objectives. For example, it is unrealistic to expect every trainee to acquire skill in radiating all possible environments.

Table 7 presents an ideal picture; in many instances, only a few of these objectives can be aimed for, or realized. Nonetheless, Table 7 provides a model for matching and coordinating the trainee's present skill level with the content of the training intervention. For example, if a trainee is lacking in discriminative skill, this component would be the initial focus of the intervention, before attempts were made to induce change in skill in radiating environments.

Trainee Characteristics

Before describing the specific trainee characteristics thought to be the most important for guiding intervention in a differential training program, it will be useful to review some underlying assumptions. A matching model framework for training teachers requires that one begin with the trainee – where he is now and his change-relevant characteristics – in order to intervene to produce change. The rationale here is identical to the belief that, in planning education intervention for the classroom, the single most important aspect is the child and "where he is now." Although the assumption that one must begin with the child is fairly obvious, and reasonably well accepted, it is less frequently assumed that one must begin with the trainee in the training of teachers. In this sense, the present model may be seen as a trainee-centered training program.

The major problem with almost every attempt to individualize instruction or to devise a person-centered educational program is the inordinately large number of individual differences which might be considered. The educational planner is overwhelmed by the myriad differences among persons, and further confused by the fact that very few of these differences are coordinated with specifically appropriate educational interventions. Faced by this double dilemma – "Every student (or trainee) is unique" and "Because of his uniqueness, every student must be treated differently" – the educational decision maker is likely to abandon all efforts toward individualization or differential treatment.

We are not concerned with cataloguing all of the ways in which trainees vary. We are concerned only with those characteristics which are systematically related to the selection of the most appropriate training intervention. Two classes of trainee characteristics will be considered: first, trainee skill level, which will be coordinated with the content of the training intervention (Chapter IV) and second, trainee accessibility characteristics, which will be coordinated with the form of the intervention (Chapter III). Put simply, if we know what he knows and can do, this prescribes what he needs to learn; if we know his modes of accessibility, this prescribes how the content should be presented. There are no doubt many other important trainee characteristics, but we will be concerned only with those which are related to differential training procedures, either theoretically or empirically. Since no program can treat every person as completely unique, the practical issue becomes what are the most important adaptations to make.

Skill level

The trainee should be characterized in terms of his present position on skill components: skill in discrimination, skill in radiating environments, and skill in flexible modulation from one environment to another. These skills, and means for assessing them, have been discussed in detail in the last chapter. What is important is to assess the trainee's present skill level so that this diagnostic information can serve to make the most effective differential placement.

Accessibility characteristics

Using Lewinian terminology, the change process is described as one of first unfreezing, producing change, and then refreezing. Viewed in such a way, the immediate problem is to specify the procedure for unfreezing or reaching the trainee. We consider this issue by characterizing trainees in terms of accessibility characteristics, just as we proposed to describe students in Chapter III. It is not sufficient to

70

describe the trainee only as he is now, on a skill component profile, and to indicate that component on which change is desired. In addition, we must characterize the trainee in terms which will be directly translatable to that mode or form of training intervention to which he will be most open or accessible. Again, the rationale for accessibility characteristics is their potential for defining the most suitable environment, in this case the form of training intervention.

Cognitive orientation

Cognitive orientation appears to be an important accessibility characteristic because it indicates how a trainee will organize and interpret his experience (that is his training intervention). Specific measures of cognitive orientation are Conceptual Level (Chapter III) and integrative complexity (Schroder, Driver, & Streufert, 1967). Conceptual Level (CL) and integrative complexity are sufficiently similar that a description of CL will convey the flavor of variation in cognitive orientation. As described earlier, CL was originally based on a theory of conceptual development which hypothesized that, under ideal training conditions, a person develops from a low level of conceptual development (low CL) in which he is cognitively simple, dependent, and not capable of generating his own concepts, to a higher CL in which he is more cognitively complex, independent, and capable of generating his own concepts. CL has been used in several investigations of trainee characteristics (Bundy, 1968; Heck, 1968; Hunt, 1970).

Motivational orientation

Motivational orientation affects preference for and reaction to different forms of feedback and reward. Praise is more effective than criticism for introverts and failure avoiders, while criticism is more effective than praise for extroverts and underachievers (Schroder & Hunt, 1957; Thompson & Hunnicutt, 1944; Van de Riet, 1964). French (1958) demonstrated that persons high in affiliation motivation solved problems more effectively under conditions of feeling oriented feedback, while persons high in achievement orientation solved problems more effectively under conditions of task oriented feedback. Similarly, Wells (1958) found that persons who were other-directed worked better under conditions of experimenter defined feedback, while inner-directed persons worked better under conditions of self defined feedback. Other studies have demonstrated the differential effects of peer approval vs. authority approval.

Value orientation

Whether trainees will be likely to learn skills designed as intervention procedures which will achieve objectives they do not believe in, or that they disagree with, is a question about which there is little evidence. However, on the basis of available information as well as intuition, it seems important to include the trainee's value orientation as a classification characteristic for differential training. Teacher trainee attitude toward the best way to teach, that is, by inductive or deductive methods, has been related to the teacher trainee's preferred style of communication (Hunt, 1970).

   In an educational context, it is probably inadvisable to use a single dimension to

71

measure a trainee's value orientation. What is probably most important for the trainee is whether he can accept a variety of procedures as being useful at different times. Unless the trainee who favors inquiry and inductive lessons can also accept the necessity for structured lessons and didactic presentation, he will be much like the "rigid liberal," and as difficult to change as a trainee with exactly the opposite values. This point was especially clear in observing some trainees in an urban teacher preparation program who valued giving students freedom, and refused to establish order in the classroom or learn procedures for doing so.

Measures of value orientation (for example Minnesota Teacher Attitude Inventory, Attitudes to Teaching, Hunt, 1970) will require revision and extension so that they do not simply classify the trainee on a single dimension. It seems necessary that they also include the person's "latitude of acceptance," or that area on the dimension to which the person is open to information.

Much of the lack of knowledge about the relation between value orientation and the acquisition of skill comes from lack of information about the role of awareness – how does explicit knowledge of one's instrumental quality affect the learning of teaching skills (see Chapter IV). As we learn about this role, we will better understand how values are likely to intrude on, or facilitate, skill acquisition. Bereiter's (1969) suggestion is appropriate in this regard:

"What we should try to do is give students the increment in IQ without all the agony of belief and disbelief that hampers its coming. This is not easy, but there is a time-honored principle that is applicable to the effort. The principle is, 'Should follows Can.' Try in every way to get students to where they have the capability of applying a new way of thinking before putting them in a position to pass judgment upon it" (p. 75).

How much it is possible to postpone the "should" question without affecting the trainee's acquisition of skills and understanding is an area which deserves much more investigation. Perhaps then we will learn the answer to the question – how does the awareness of what you are doing affect your learning to do it?

Another factor linking value orientation and skill acquisition is the trainee's feeling of adequacy. One reason for a trainee's disinclination to acquire a skill which is at odds with his present value orientation may be the threat that learning this skill would pose to his feelings of adequacy.

Sensory orientation

Most forms of presentation in training intervention involve both visual and auditory spheres. However, in some instances, there may be an option, and it seems useful to consider the trainee's preferred sensory modality.

Summary of trainee characteristics

First, the trainee should be characterized in relation to his position on the skill level in question, for example, if the objective is skill in discriminating between environments, then his level on this component should be assessed. If he is weak on the component, then consideration must be given to his accessibility to intervention aimed toward increasing his skill level. To do this, he should be characterized

72

according to an accessibility profile: cognitive orientation (Conceptual Level, or the complexity with which he processes information); motivational orientation (importance of certain interpersonal needs); value orientation (his position and "latitude of acceptance" on relevant dimensions); and sensory orientation (preference for visual or auditory presentation).

Training Intervention Characteristics

A trainee centered program requires procedures appropriate to the trainee. Taken literally, the training program would be developed on the basis of trainee characteristics after the trainees had been selected. Although such literal adaption is clearly impossible, the training program must be kept flexible with numerous options available.

Planning a training program with flexible options for intervention sounds like a reasonable idea; however, the implications of such flexible planning should be briefly considered. Frequently, new training programs seem to be built around the most popular new form of training as their central single feature, such as T-group sensitivity training, or video feedback; but a differential training program cannot be fixed to a single procedure in an across-the-board fashion. This is not to say that equipment for video feedback training should not be available in a differential training program, but rather that such equipment should be regarded as one of the many resources available for accomplishing certain training objectives with certain trainees.

Perhaps the most difficult feature in adopting a flexible program is that program planners have to forego the security of a fixed four year or one year curriculum outline. Also the staff in such a program will never be quite sure what forms of training they will have to provide in the future.

Cronbach (1967) has made an interesting suggestion in this regard:

"I suggest that we set out to invent interactions. Specifically, we ought to take a differential variable we think promising and design alternative treatments to interact with that variable" (p. 32).

The logic for selecting the following intervention characteristics follows Cronbach's rationale, in that only those program features directly related to variation among trainees are discussed. Variations in training procedures, therefore, are considered in two general categories, content and form, which are related to the two trainee categories, skill level and accessibility characteristics.

Content of intervention

Training procedures designed to produce the objectives in Table 7 are described in Chapter IV. A major value of the skill-content matching model in Table 7 is to define that specific content which a trainee needs to learn; thus, if he is deficient in the capacity to discriminate between environments, he should be trained in this area.

Form of intervention

Among the countless variations in intervention procedures, only those dimensions will be considered which are related to trainee accessibility characteristics, and these we summarized in Table 6.

Structure of presentation

Structural variation includes both the structured-flexible dimension, or the degree to which the trainee can interact responsively with the material, and the degree of organizational complexity of the material. Short-term structural variation is exemplified by variations in rule-example sequencing, in which the example-only form represents low structure, while the rule-example form represents high structure. Structural variation over a longer time period is represented by variation from the low structure of a discovery approach to the high structure of a lecture approach; from independent study to highly organized study; and from student centered approaches to teacher centered approaches.

Several examples of measuring the intervention procedures in terms of their degree of structure are available: environmental complexity (Schroder, Driver, & Streufert, 1967); structured-flexible programs (Hunt & Hardt, 1967a); and reflective environments (Hunt & Joyce, 1967).

Form of feedback and reward

A trainee may receive information about his performance in many different forms. For example, he may receive feedback directly through self-viewing on video, or he may simply be told about his performance. The source of feedback may vary: he can be informed by his supervisor or he can be informed by his fellow trainees (authority-peer variation).

Reward may vary not only in its nature (positive-negative), its source (authority-peer), but in its informational quality (informational-approval). Informational reward, for example, "that's right", is essentially identical to feedback, while reward in the form of approval ("I like the way you're doing that"), carries information only about the source's evaluation, not about trainee performance.

Value context of presentation

A matching model should specify the optimal disparity between the trainee's orientation and the presentation, as described in Chapter I. Ordinarily, the most effective training presentation is neither identical to the trainee's present position, nor too disparate from it. Rather, it should be close to his present position, within his "latitude of acceptance."

In some cases it may be possible to maintain a "value-neutral" context. If skill acquisition requires some involvement and affective arousal, however, the positioning of the presentation on a value dimension becomes important. Although forms of training intervention have not typically been considered on specific attitudinal dimensions, it should be helpful to view various interventions as either "absolute," in that presentation differs in a predetermined amount from the trainee's position, or "gradual," in that presentation begins at apoint very close to that of the trainee's position, and gradually deviates from that point (Harvey & Rutherford, 1958).

74

Modality of presentation
Variation in modality has become more apparent with the increased use of video feedback and films, which usually provide both self viewing and self listening. Little is known about the general or differential effects of multimodality (self viewing and listening) vs. single modality (only self listening); the distinctions should be made in intervention procedures when possible so that such information can be accrued.

Relation between Trainee Accessibility Characteristics and Form of Intervention

Having described the variations in trainee characteristics and intervention procedures, we now consider how specific trainee characteristics can be used to determine the most specifically appropriate training intervention. Table 8 contains the relations described in Table 6, but adds specific examples. Since Table 8 considers only the most effective form in which the content is presented, it is assumed that the content has already been matched to trainee skill level, according to Table 7.

Table 8 / Training Intervention Based on Trainee Accessibility Characteristics

Accessibility characteristic	Prescribed form of intervention
Cognitive orientation	*Degree of structure*
Low Conceptual level	High
High Conceptual level	Low or intermediate
Motivational orientation	*Form of feedback and reward*
High social approval	Extrinsic reward and/or normative feedback
High intrinsic motivation	Intrinsic reward and/or self-defined feedback
Value orientation	*Value context of presentation*
	Within "latitude of acceptance"
Sensory orientation	*Modality of presentation*
	Adapted to primary sensory "channel"
	i.e. visual, auditory

In what follows, the principles for prescribing the best intervention for an individual trainee are derived. Issues such as grouping and how many trainees to put together, will not be considered, since these issues frequently depend upon available resources, and the urgency for change. Many of the examples of differential effects are from areas other than the training of training agents, because the differential approach has not been used that frequently in training; however, the same principles should apply.

Relation between trainee cognitive orientation and structure of presentation
The structure of the presentation should be modulated to the trainee's conceptual complexity, or CL (Chapter III): the higher the trainee's CL, the more likely he is to be accessible through a more complex presentation or one which is interdependent; conversely, low CL trainees are likely to be more accessible through a

75

more structured, less complex presentation. Bundy (1968) found, in training educational administrators to make more effective decisions, that high CL administrators were adversely affected by a structured guide, while those lower in CL tended to profit from the structured guide. Heck (1968) found in training to increase communication skill, that high CL trainees profited more from the unstructured form of sensitivity training while low CL trainees profited more from a more structured human relations training program.

Relation between trainee motivational orientation and form of feedback and reward
Self-viewing, or video feedback, has recently become a frequently employed device in teacher training programs, and its effectiveness also depends upon trainee characteristics, as Salomon and McDonald (1970) stated:

"... *reactions to self-viewing of one's teaching performance on video tape are determined largely by the viewer's predispositions. That is, his satisfaction with his own performance determines what will be noticed on the screen, how it will be evaluated, and to what attitudinal change it will lead*" (p. 285).

These authors reported more specifically that teacher trainees who were dissatisfied with their teaching performance and low in self-esteem, when compared with more satisfied, high self-esteem trainees, were less favorable in their attitudes toward teaching after self-viewing. The low self-esteem trainees were also more likely to attend more to physical cues of their appearance. In contrast, trainees who were more satisfied, and had a higher self-esteem, improved their self-evaluation, and were more likely to attend to cues related to their teaching performance.

Several examples of the motivational orientation-feedback relation were described earlier, for example persons high in affiliation functioned more effectively with feeling-oriented feedback, and persons high in achievement orientation functioned better with task-oriented feedback (French, 1958). Whether the feedback or evaluation comes from an authority figure, for example, a supervising teacher, or from a peer is especially relevant in teacher training. Harvey's finding (1964) that persons high in affiliation were more accessible through peer-based statements while authoritarian persons were more accessible through authority-based statements illustrates such a differential effect.

Relation between trainee value orientation and the value context of presentation
To specify the precise optimal distance between the training presentation and the trainee's present position on the value dimension is complicated by factors such as the trainee's latitude of acceptance and his intensity of belief. However, Harvey & Rutherford (1958) found that the absolute approach was more effective with authoritarian persons, while the gradual approach was more effective with non-authoritarian persons.

In another attitude change study, McClintock (1958) found that persons high in other-directedness were more susceptible to an informational approach than to an approach aimed to give them insight into their attitudes. The insight approach, however, was found to be effective with persons moderate or low in ego defense. These investigations need to be extended to the training domain, so that we can

76

learn more about the limiting or facilitating effects of various training procedures upon trainees with varying value orientations.

Relation between trainee sensory orientation and modality of presentation
This form of differential training effectiveness is nicely illustrated by studies investigating the effect of filmed intervention as compared with other forms of instruction. Snow, Tiffin & Seibert (1965) summarized their findings as follows:

"Thus, ascendant, assertive individuals and individuals who are relatively irresponsible apparently do not learn as well from films as they do from live presentations. When shown in darkened rooms without provision for active student participation, films may foster a spectator attitude which, while having a deleterious effect on the learning of active, assertive students, may be comfortable for their more submissive peers. Possibly, film provides an atmosphere in which the more interpersonal attitudes of responsibility and conscientiousness are required while self-assertiveness is frustrated" (p. 320).

An investigation by Koran, McDonald & Snow (1969) on the differential effects of film mediated modeling compared with written modeling is also relevant. They reported that, while video modeling was more effective for trainees who were relatively low in analytic ability and high in visual memory, the written modeling intervention was more effective for trainees who were highly analytic but low in visual memory.

Illustrative Application of the Model: Increasing Flexibility in Teaching
To give an example of how the matching models might be used, let us consider how they might be applied in a specific case: increasing teaching flexibility. Flexibility in teaching is, in many ways, like creativity in the learner: both are value-laden, generally desirable states which are usually poorly specified and given inadequate operational definitions.

In defining teaching flexibility, we follow Joyce and Hodges (1966), who stated in their discussion of instructional flexibility training that "a teacher who can purposefully exhibit a wide range of teaching styles is potentially able to accomplish more than a teacher whose repertoire is relatively limited" (p. 409). Their definition of flexibility includes only the capacity to radiate a wide variety of environments, and does not explicitly include their use under differentially appropriate circumstances, as described in Table 7. However, we take this simpler definition of flexibility because it is clearly a prerequisite to a more comprehensive form of flexibility.

This definition does not refer to the stimulus situation (variation in learners) in which the variation in response (radiating an environment) occurs. Scott's (1966) critical analysis of the terms flexibility, rigidity and adaptation from a stimulus-response view can be applied to flexibility in teaching behavior. Scott criticized the unqualified endorsement of flexibility as always desirable. He classified forms of response variation by noting its relation to stimulus variation, or in teaching terms, variation in teaching behavior as a function of variation in student behavior. "Stimulus tracking" refers to response variation which is completely determined by stimulus variation (teacher changes procedures whenever students change), while "spontaneous alternation" refers to response variation which is unrelated to stimulus variation (teacher changes procedure for no apparent reason). He pointed out that neither adaptation nor flexibility, can be adequately defined only in terms of simply spontaneous variation nor in terms of stimulus tracking. Scott concludes by noting the following:

"It is possible that adaptation may best be facilitated if the person conceives of his various requirements in a hierarchy of importance, treating some of them as 'goals' or 'ultimate values' and others as 'means'. The constancy or 'rigidity' may be adopted with respect to the goals, and flexibility with respect to the means. In terms of our behavior categories, this is to say that modification of the environment to meet the person's requirements is best accomplished if behavior patterns expressing ultimate goals are maintained relatively fixed in the face of changing circumstances, while means-relevant behavior patterns display spontaneous variability and stimulus tracking" (p. 397).

While teaching flexibility requires skill in using a variety of teaching environments, we consider only two in the present example, structured and reflective, or interdependent teaching (Hunt & Joyce, 1967). The first step in applying the model to this objective, therefore, is to assess the trainee's present skill level, to determine whether he can radiate the same material in both a reflective and structured context. Assuming that the trainee cannot radiate one or both these environments (but is capable of making the prerequisite discriminations in Table 7), we consider how to apply the models to planning such trainee-specific intervention.

Planning content of intervention
One example of the content for inducing two kinds of teaching is found in a study by Shaver (1964), who attempted to induce the teacher's adoption of Socratic and recitation styles, which are generally similar to reflective and structured environments. Shaver defined the intervention as follows:

"The orientation of the teachers involved several steps: (1) General discussion of the two teaching styles as an integral part of the total research project; (2) the reading of a theoretical description of the two styles; (3) a session of approximately two hours spent in discussing points which needed clarification and problems which might arise in applying the theoretical models in the classroom situation; and (4) impromptu conferences after teaching periods to discuss specific problems which occurred in attempting to conform to the teaching styles" (p. 260).

Planning form of presentation

Structure of presentation
If the trainee's cognitive orientation is relatively simple (low CL), then the material should be presented in simple, concrete form, for example by providing typescripts or clear demonstrations from which the trainee can model. If the trainee's cognitive orientation is more complex, then the material should be organized in more abstract conceptual form such as a theoretical rationale for procedure.

78

Form of feedback and reward

If the trainee is more susceptible to peer influence than authority influence, the procedure should be adapted accordingly. The trainee who is rigidly adherent only to reflective teaching might be given student feedback indicating its lack of effectiveness. For example, an intervention procedure might be designed in which the trainee's task was to teach a student a particular skill which could be taught only through a structured procedure. The intervention procedure might then be programmed so that the student would not learn unless the trainee employed a structured procedure.

Value context of presentation

Since there is a relation between value orientation and preferred teaching style (Hunt, 1970), a trainee capable of radiating only one environment, such as reflective approach, is likely to have a negative attitude toward the other environment. This negative attitude toward structured teaching is especially likely to occur in trainees classified as "weak-sensitive" (Hunt, 1970), or those who believe the only teaching approach is a reflective, open environment. Such trainees are unlikely to acquire skill in structured teaching through a "value neutral" approach, in which it is a skill to be acquired, with no questions asked. However, if a "gradual" approach is used so that the trainee gradually becomes aware of the possible usefulness of structured teaching, this is more likely to produce the desired results.

Modality of presentation

Studies such as those by Snow, Tiffin, & Seibert (1965), and Koran, McDonald, & Snow (1969) will be helpful in guiding these decisions. Special attention should be focussed on trainee characteristics associated with susceptibility to multi-modal approaches, as distinct from single modality of presentation.

Student Effect on Teaching Behavior

Whether a teacher adopts a reflective or structured approach also depends on the students he is teaching. However, we tend to consider the effect in only one direction, that of the teacher on the student. Bell proposed (1968) a "direction of effects" model for analyzing parent-child interaction which emphasizes that the child "pulls" different parental responses just as the parent affects the child. In the classroom, direction of effects simply emphasizes the common sense notion that the students affect the teacher's behavior (Turner, 1967).

How the student's CL affects the teaching method used by teachers, also varying in CL, was investigated by Rathbone (1970). Twenty experienced teachers were classified into a low and a high CL group, and eighty sixth grade students were classified as low or high CL, and then assigned in groups of four to each teacher. Assignments were made so that half the high CL teachers taught low CL students and half of the low CL teachers taught high CL students. Teachers' behavior was recorded, and coded according to the proportion of interdependent communications (those statements which help students to theorize or think for themselves, Joyce & Harootunian, 1967). The proportion of interdependent communications was also the measure of reflective teaching in the study described in Chapter IV by Hunt & Joyce (1967) which reported that high CL teacher trainees were more likely to adopt a reflective teaching method. Results from the Rathbone study extend the Hunt-Joyce findings to student effects, and are summarized in Table 9.

Table 9 / Proportion of Interdependent Teaching as a Function of Teacher and Student CL[a]

Student CL	Teacher CL Low	High	Total
Low	.059	.124	.096
High	.126	.264	.203
Total	.093	.195	.149

[a](after Rathbone, 1970)

The teacher effects reported in Table 9 replicate the Hunt-Joyce results ($F = 12.02, p < .01$). However, more relevant to the present topic is the result that student CL is an equally important influence ($F = 12.37, p < .01$) in determining the proportion of interdependent communications, or reflective teaching. It should also be noted that low CL teachers modulated to student CL as much as did high CL teachers. In both teacher groups, the incidence of reflective teaching is approximately twice as great for high CL students as for low CL students. Results in Table 9 are an excellent example of direction of effects between teachers and students varying in CL.

Limiting Factors in the Use of Matching Models
Matching is useful only when certain trainee characteristics interact with modes of intervention in producing the objective. As Cronbach (1967) puts it:

"Aptitude information is not useful in adapting instruction unless the aptitude and treatment interact — more specifically, unless the regression line relating aptitude to payoff under one treatment crosses the regression line for the competing treatment" (p. 30).

For example, Schroder and Talbot (1966), in attempting to increase teaching flexibility through two forms of intervention concluded that their results:

"... indicated that the ability to sense and utilize another person's perspective in communication is a relatively stable personality characteristic which persists despite short-term lecture and video feedback training methods" (p. 12).

Experimental studies investigating the validity of the present matching models, especially the relation between skill acquisition and accessibility characteristics, will therefore not only need to control for initial trainee skill level, but will also need to partial out the initial relation between the trainee accessibility characteristic and skill level. In other words, more investigations are required into correlates of what Lewin (1936) called plasticity, "the ease with which a relatively lasting and stable change can be made in the structure of a region" (pp. 161-162).

Matching models are only general guides for planning intervention at a particular time, and must be continually updated to index any changes in the trainee. Different

80

approaches may be required for the same trainee at different times, because for example the trainee's motivational orientation may change over time.

It is frequently observed that the introduction of an educational innovation is relatively easy, but providing conditions under which the innovation will be maintained is very difficult. Probably the most underemphasized reason for this difficulty lies in the training agent's motivational orientation, especially his need for novelty. These factors of the teacher's motivational orientation are especially important in planning in-service training programs.

The prescriptions in the models for deriving trainee-specific intervention vary in their empirical support. Therefore, the models should be regarded only as provisional statements which will permit empirical exploration into the problem of developing more effective differential training programs for the training of teachers.

REFERENCES

ASTROVE, G. Preference for educational environments as a function of student conceptual level. Unpublished honors thesis, Syracuse University, 1966.

AUSUBEL, D. P. *Theory and problems of child development.* New York: Grune & Stratton, 1958.

BANDURA, A. Behavioral modification through modeling procedures. In Krasner, L. & Ullmann, L. P. (Eds.), *Research in behavior modification.* New York: Holt, Rinehart, & Winston, 1965.

BANDURA, A., & MCDONALD, F. J. Influence of social reinforcement and the behavior of models in shaping children's moral judgments. *Journal of Abnormal and Social Psychology,* 1963, **67**, 274-281.

BELL, R. Q. A reinterpretation of the direction of effects in studies of socialization. *Psychological Review,* 1968, **75**, 81-95.

BEREITER, C. Commentary. In Herbert, J. & Ausubel, D. P. (Eds.), *Psychology in teacher preparation.* Toronto: Ontario Institute for Studies in Education, 1969. Pp. 73-76.

BETTELHEIM, B. How much can man change? *New York Review of Books,* September 10, 1964, **3**, 1-4.

BLOOM, B. S. (Ed.) *Taxonomy of educational objectives.* New York: David McKay, 1956.

BRADFORD, L. P., GIBB, J. R. & BENNE, K. D. *T-group theory and laboratory methods: innovation in re-education.* New York: Wiley, 1964.

BRIM, O. G. *Education for child rearing.* New York: Russell Sage, 1959.

BROGAN, D. W. *America in the modern world.* Rutgers University Press, New Brunswick, New Jersey, 1960.

BROOKS, E. D. The effect of alternative techniques for modifying teacher behavior. Unpublished doctoral dissertation, Stanford University, 1967.

BRUNER, J. C. (Ed.) *The process of education.* Cambridge: Harvard University Press, 1960.

BUNDY, R. F. An investigation into the use of a programmed guide on the effectiveness of problem analysis behavior in public school administrators. Unpublished doctoral dissertation, Syracuse University, 1968.

CAMPBELL, D. T. Recommendations for APA test standards regarding construct, trait, or discriminant validity. *American Psychologist,* 1960, **15**, 546-553.

CAMPBELL, D. T. Conformity in psychology's theories of acquired behavioral dispositions. In Berg, I. A. & Bass, B. M. (Eds.), *Conformity and deviation.* New York: Harper, 1961. Pp. 101-142.

CARR, J. E. The role of conceptual organization in interpersonal discrimination. *Journal of Psychology,* 1965, **59**, 159-176.

CLAUNCH, N. Cognitive and motivational characteristics associated with concrete and abstract levels of conceptual complexity. Unpublished doctoral dissertation, Princeton University, 1964.

CRANDALL, V. C., CRANDALL, V. J., & KATKOVSKY, W. A children's social desirability questionnaire. *Journal of Consulting Psychology,* 1965, **29**, 27-36.

CRONBACH, L. J. The two disciplines of scientific psychology. *American Psychologist,* 1957, **12**, 671-684.

CRONBACH, L. J. How can instruction be adapted to individual differences. In R. M. Gagné (Ed.), *Learning and individual differences.* New York: Macmillan, 1967. Pp. 23-44.

CRONBACH, L. J., & SNOW, R. E. Project on individual differences in learning ability as a function of instructional variables. Annual Report No. 2, 1968, U.S. Office of Education, Contract No. OEC 4-6-061269-1217, School of Education, Stanford University.

CRONBACH, L. J., & SNOW, R. E. Individual differences in learning ability as a function of instructional variables. Final Report, 1969, School of Education, Stanford University.

CROSS, H. J. The relation of parental training conditions to conceptual level in adolescent boys. *Journal of Personality,* 1966, **34**, 348-365.

CROSS, H. J. The relation of parental training to conceptual structure in pre-adolescents. *Journal of Genetic Psychology*, 1970, **116**, 197-202.

DAVITZ, J. *The communication of emotional meaning.* New York: McGraw-Hill, 1964.

DEUTSCH, M. Social intervention and the malleability of the child. In Deutsch, M. (Ed.), *The disadvantaged child.* New York: Basic Books, 1967.

DEWEY, J. *The child and the curriculum.* Chicago: University of Chicago Press, 1902.

FESTINGER, L. *A theory of cognitive dissonance.* Stanford: Stanford University Press, 1957.

FLAVELL, J. H. in collaboration with Patricia C. Botkin (and others). *The development of role taking and communication skills in children.* New York: Wiley, 1968.

FRANCE, S. A. A comparison of integration level theory and conceptual systems theory using a delinquent population. Unpublished master's thesis, Syracuse University, 1968.

FROMM, E. *Escape from freedom.* New York: Rinehart, 1941.

FRENCH, E. G. Effects of the interaction of motivation and feedback on task performance. In Atkinson, J. W. (Ed.), *Motives in fantasy, action, and society.* Princeton, N.J.: Van Nostrand, 1958. Pp. 400-408.

GASSNER, S. M. The relationship between patient-therapist compatibility and treatment effectiveness. Unpublished doctoral dissertation, Syracuse University, 1968.

GOLDSTEIN, A. P., HELLER, K., & SECHREST, L. B. *Psychotherapy and the psychology of behavior change.* New York: Wiley, 1966.

GOLLIN, E. S. Organizational characteristics of social judgment: A developmental investigation. *Journal of Personality*, 1958, **26**, 139-154.

GRANT, M. Q., WARREN, M., & TURNER, J. K. Community treatment project: An evaluation of community treatment for delinquents. CTP Research Report No. 3, California Youth Authority, Sacramento, California, 1963.

HARRISON, R., & OSHRY, B. I. The impact of laboratory training on organizational behavior: Methodology and results. Mimeographed technical report, 1967, National Training Laboratories, Washington, D.C.

HARVEY, O. J. Some cognitive determinants of influenceability. *Sociometry*, 1964, **27**, 208-221.

HARVEY O. J. Conceptual systems and attitude change. In Sherif, C. W., & Sherif, M. (Eds.), *Attitude, ego-involvement, and change.* New York: Wiley, 1967. Pp. 201-226.

HARVEY, O. J., HUNT, D. E., & SCHRODER, H. M. *Conceptual systems and personality organization.* New York: Wiley, 1961.

HARVEY, O. J., & RUTHERFORD, J. Gradual and absolute approaches to attitude change. *Sociometry*, 1958, **21**, 61-68.

HARVEY, O. J., & SCHRODER, H. M. Cognitive aspects of self and motivation. In Harvey, O. J. (Ed.), *Motivation and social interaction: Cognitive determinants.* New York: Ronald, 1963. Pp. 95-133.

HECK, E. J. A study concerning the differential effectiveness of two approaches to human relationship training in facilitating change in interpersonal communication skill and style of interpersonal perception. Unpublished doctoral dissertation, Syracuse University, 1968.

HUNT, D. E. Modification of conceptual development. Paper presented at the meeting of the Society for Research in Child Development, State College, Pennsylvania, 1961.

HUNT, D. E. Personality patterns of adolescent boys. Progress Report, National Institute of Mental Health, Bethesda, Maryland, 1962.

HUNT, D. E. Personality patterns of adolescent boys. Progress Report, 1964, National Institute of Mental Health, Bethesda, Maryland, 1964.

HUNT, D. E. Indicators of developmental change in lower class children. United States Office of Education Report, Washington, D.C., 1965. (a)

HUNT, D. E. A component pre-training assessment program for Peace Corps Trainees in Tanzania X. Unpublished manuscript, Syracuse University, 1965. (b)

HUNT, D. E. Adolescence: Cultural deprivation, poverty, and the dropout. *Review of Educational Research*, 1966, **36**, 463-473.

HUNT, D. E. Longitudinal analysis of conceptual level scores. Unpublished manuscript, Syracuse University, 1968.

HUNT, D. E. Adaptability in interpersonal communication among training agents. *The Merrill-Palmer Quarterly of Behavior and Development*, 1970, **16**.

HUNT, D. E., & DOPYERA, J. Indicators of developmental change in lower class children. Interim Progress Report, 1963, Youth Development Center, Syracuse University.

HUNT, D. E., & DOPYERA, J. Indicators of developmental change in lower class children. Second Interim Report, 1964, Youth Development Center, Syracuse University.

HUNT, D. E., & DOPYERA, J. Personality variation in lower-class children. *Journal of Psychology*, 1966, **62**, 47-54.

HUNT, D. E., & HARDT, R. H. Developmental stage, delinquency, and differential treatment. *Journal of Research in Crime and Delinquency*, 1965, **2**, 20-31.

HUNT, D. E., & HARDT, R. H. Characterization of 1966 Summer Upward Bound Program. Syracuse University Youth Development Center, 1967. (a)

HUNT, D. E., & HARDT, R. H. The role of conceptual level and program structure in Summer Upward Bound Programs. Paper presented at the meeting of the Eastern Psychological Association, Boston, April, 1967. (b)

HUNT, D. E., HARDT, R. H., & VICTOR, J. B. Characterization of Upward Bound: Summer and academic year 1967-1968. Syracuse University Youth Development Center, 1968.

HUNT, D. E., & JOYCE, B. R. Teacher trainee personality and initial teaching style. *American Educational Research Journal*, 1967, **4**, 253-259.

HUNT, D. E., JOYCE, B. R., & DELPOPOLO, J. An exploratory study in the modification of students' teaching patterns. Unpublished manuscript, Syracuse University, 1964.

HUNT, D. E., LAPIN, S., LIBERMAN, B., MCMANUS, J., POST, R., SABALIS, R., SWEET, S., & VICTOR, J. B. Manual for coding paragraph completion responses for adolescents. Unpublished manuscript, Syracuse University Youth Development Center, 1968.

HUNT, D. E., & MCMANUS, J. M. Preliminary investigation of boys known to probation. Final Report, January, 1968. Office of Law Enforcement Assistance, Washington, D.C.

HUNT, J. MCV. *Intelligence and experience.* New York: Ronald, 1961.

JOYCE, B. R. A manual for coding teacher communications relevant to conceptual systems theory. Unpublished manuscript, University of Chicago, 1964.

JOYCE, B. R. Method and methods in teacher education: Geist, form, and substance. *Journal of Teacher Education*, 1969, **20**, 509-520.

JOYCE, B. R., & HAROOTUNIAN, B. *The structure of teaching.* Chicago: Science Research Associates, 1967.

JOYCE, B. R., & HODGES, R. E. Instructional flexibility training. *Journal of Teacher Education*, 1966, **17**, 409-416.

KAGAN, J. On the need for relativism. *American Psychologist*, 1967, **22**, 131-142.

KAHN, R. L., & CANNELL, C. F. *The dynamics of interviewing.* New York: Wiley, 1957.

KATZ, I. The socialization of academic motivation in minority group children. In *Nebraska symposium on motivation.* Lincoln: University of Nebraska Press, 1967. Pp. 133-191.

KELMAN, H. C. Processes of opinion change. *Public Opinion Quarterly*, 1961, **25**, 57-79.

KELMAN, H. C. The role of the group in the induction of therapeutic change. *International Journal of Group Psychotherapy*, 1963, **13**, 399-432.

KOHLBERG, L. The development of children's orientation toward a moral order: I. Sequence in the development of moral thought. *Vita Humana*, 1963, **6**, 11-33.

KOHLBERG, L. Relationships between the development of moral judgement and moral conduct. Paper presented at the meeting of the Society for Research in Child Development, Minneapolis, Minnesota, 1965.

KOHLBERG, L. Moral education in the schools: a developmental view. *School Review*, 1966, **74**, 1-30.

KOHNSTAMM, G. A. Experiments on teaching Piagetian thought operations. Paper presented at the Conference on Guided Learning. Cleveland, Ohio, January 1966.

KORAN, M. L., MCDONALD, F. J., & SNOW, R. E. The effects of individual differences on observational learning in the acquisition of a teaching skill. Paper presented at American Educational Research Association, Los Angeles, California, 1969.

KRATHWOHL, D., BLOOM, B. B., & MASIA, B. B. *Taxonomy of educational objectives: Handbook II. Affective domain.* New York: David McKay, 1964.

LEWIN, K. *A dynamic theory of personality.* New York: McGraw-Hill, 1935.

LEWIN, K. *Principles of topological psychology.* New York: McGraw-Hill, 1936.

LIPPITT, R., WATSON, J., & WESTLEY, B. *The dynamics of planned change.* New York: Harcourt Brace, 1958.

LOEVINGER, J. The meaning and measurement of ego development. *American Psychologist,* 1966, **21**, 195-206.

MCCLINTOCK, C. G. Personality syndromes and attitude change. *Journal of Personality,* 1958, **26**, 479-493.

MCLACHLAN, J. F. C. Individual differences and teaching methods in student interpretation of modern art. Unpublished master's thesis, University of Toronto, 1969.

MOORE, O. K. Autotelic responsive environments and exceptional children. In Harvey, O. J. (Ed.), *Experience, structure, & adaptability.* New York: Springer, 1966. Pp. 169-216.

ONTARIO DEPARTMENT OF EDUCATION. *Living and Learning.* Report of the Provincial Committee on Aims and Objectives of Education in the Schools of Ontario. Toronto: Ontario Department of Education, 1968.

PALMER, T. B. An overview of matching in the Community Treatment Project. Paper presented at the meeting of the Western Psychological Association, San Diego, California, 1968.

PERVIN, L. A. Performance and satisfaction as a function of individual-environment fit. *Psychological Bulletin,* 1968, **69**, 56-68.

PIAGET, J. *The moral judgment of the child.* London: Routledge & Kegan Paul, 1932.

POHL, R. L., & PERVIN, L. A. Academic performance as a function of task requirements and cognitive style. *Psychological Reports,* 1968, **22**, 1017-1020.

RATHBONE, C. Teachers' information handling behavior when grouped with students by Conceptual Level. Unpublished doctoral dissertation, Syracuse University, 1970.

RIESSMAN, F. *The culturally deprived child.* New York: Harper, 1962.

ROTTER, J. B. Generalized expectancies for internal versus external control of reinforcement. *Psychological Monographs,* 1966, **80**, (1, Whole No. 609).

SALOMON, G., & MCDONALD, F. J. Pretest and posttest reactions to self-viewing one's teaching performance on video tape. *Journal of Educational Psychology,* 1970, **61**, 280-286.

SANFORD, R. N. Will psychologists study human problems? *American Psychologist,* 1965, **20**, 192-202.

SAPOLSKY, A. Relationship between patient-doctor compatibility, mutual perception, and outcome of treatment. *Journal of Abnormal Psychology,* 1965, **70**, 70-76.

SCHRODER, H. M. The measurement and development of management information systems. Invited address, International Symposium on Management Information on Systems – a challenge to scientific research, Kolan, Germany, 1970.

SCHRODER, H. M., DRIVER, M., & STREUFERT, S. *Human information processing.* New York: Holt, Rinehart, & Winston, 1967.

SCHRODER, H. M., & HUNT, D. E. Failure-avoidance in situational interpretation and problem solving. *Psychological Monographs,* 1957, **71**, (3, Whole No. 432).

SCHRODER, H. M., & TALBOT, T. The effectiveness of video feedback in sensitivity training. Report submitted to Peace Corps, Princeton University, 1966.

SCHUTZ, W. C. *FIRO.* New York: Holt, Rinehart, & Winston, 1958.

SCOTT, W. A. Flexibility, rigidity, and adaptability. Toward clarification of concepts. In Harvey, O. J. (Ed.), *Experience, structure, and adaptability,* New York: Springer, 1966. Pp. 369-400.

SHAVER, J. P. The ability of teachers to conform to two styles of teaching. *Journal of Experimental Education*, 1964, **32**, 259-267.

SMEDSLUND, J. Educational psychology. *Annual Review of Psychology*, 1964, **15**, 251-276.

SNOW, R. E. Research on media and attitudes. Paper given at conference on research on instructional media. Indiana University, Bloomington, Indiana, June 1969.

SNOW, R. E., TIFFIN, J., & SEIBERT, W. F. Individual differences and instructional effects. *Journal of Educational Psychology*, 1965, **56**, 315-326.

SROLE, L. Social integration and certain corollaries: an exploratory study. *American Sociological Review*, 1956, **21**, 709-716.

STERN, G. G. Environments for learning. In Sanford, N. (Ed.), *The American college*. New York: Wiley, 1962. Pp. 690-730.

STERN, G. G. *People in context: Measuring person-environment congruence in business and industry*. New York: Wiley, 1970.

STRODTBECK, F. L. Family interaction, values and achievement. In McClelland, D. C. *et al.* (Eds.), *Talent and society*. New York: Van Nostrand, 1958. Pp. 137-194.

STUEMPFIG, D. W., & MAEHR, M. L. The effects of conceptual structure and personal quality of feedback on motivation. *Child Development*, 1970, **41**.

SUCHMAN, R. J. Inquiry training: building skills for autonomous discovery. *The Merrill-Palmer Quarterly of Behavior and Development*, 1961, **7**, 147-170.

SULLIVAN, C. E., GRANT, M. Q., & GRANT, J. D. The development of interpersonal maturity: Application to delinquency. *Psychiatry*, 1957, **20**, 373-385.

SULLIVAN, E. V., MCCULLOUGH, G., & STAGER, M. A developmental study of the relation between conceptual, ego, and moral development. *Child Development*, 1970, **41**, 399-412.

THELEN, H. A. *Classroom grouping for teachability*. New York: Wiley, 1967.

THOMPSON, G. G., & HUNNICUTT, C. W. The effect of repeated praise or blame on the work achievement of "introverts" and "extroverts." *Journal of Educational Psychology*, 1944, **30**, 75-85.

TOMKINS, S. S., & MINER, J. B. *The Tomkins-Horn picture arrangement test*. New York: Springer, 1957.

TOMLINSON, P. D. Differential effectiveness of three teaching strategies for students of varying conceptual levels. Unpublished master's thesis, University of Toronto, 1969.

TORRANCE, E. P. Different ways of learning for different kinds of children. In Torrance, E. P., & Strom, R. D. (Eds.), *Mental health and achievement: Increasing potential and reducing school dropout*. New York: Wiley, 1965. Pp. 253-262.

TRUAX, C. B., & CARKHUFF, R. R. *Toward effective counseling and psychotherapy: training and practice*. Chicago: Aldine, 1967.

TUCKMAN, B. W. A study of the effectiveness of directive vs nondirective vocational teachers as a function of student characteristics and course format. Final Report U.S. Office of Education, Washington, D.C. 1968.

TURIEL, E. An experimental test of the sequentiality of developmental stages in the child's moral judgments. *Journal of Personality and Social Psychology*, 1966, **3**, 611-618.

TURIEL, E. Developmental processes in the child's moral thinking. In Mussen, P., Langer, J., & Covington, M. (Eds.), *Trends and issues in developmental psychology*. New York: Holt, Rinehart, & Winston, 1969. Pp. 92-133.

TURNER, R. Pupil influence on teacher behavior. *Classroom Interaction Newsletter*, 1967, **3**, 5-8.

VAN DE RIET, H. Effects of praise and reproof on paired-associate learning in educationally retarded children. *Journal of Educational Psychology*, 1964, **55**, 139-143.

WARREN, M. Q. Classification of offenders as an aid to efficient management and effective treatment. Community Treatment Project. Prepared for President's Commission on law enforcement and administration of justice. Task force on correction, Washington, D.C. 1966.

WARREN, M. Q. The Community Treatment Project after five years. California Youth Authority, Sacramento, California, 1967.

WARREN, M. Q., & COMMUNITY TREATMENT PROJECT STAFF. Interpersonal maturity level classification. Juvenile, 1966 Ed. California Youth Authority, 1966.

WASHBOURNE, C., & HEIL, L. N. What characteristics of teachers affect children's growth? *School Review*, 1960, **68**, 420-426.

WEINSTEIN, G. A method for assessing ability to control and regulate classroom behavior. Unpublished manuscript, Syracuse University, 1965.

WELLS, H. H. The role of two processes in determining reactions to two forms of failure stimulation. Unpublished manuscript. Yale University, 1958.

WOHLWILL, J. F. The teaching machine: Psychology's new hobbyhorse. *Teachers College Record*, 1962, **64**, 139-146.

WOLFE, R. The role of conceptual systems in cognitive functioning at varying levels of age and intelligence. *Journal of Personality*, 1963, **31**, 108-123.